Architecture and Plurality

ARCHITECTURE AND PLURALITY

Edited by Mohsen Mostafavi

Lars Müller Publishers

AGA KHAN AWARD
FOR ARCHITECTURE

Preface

Farrokh Derakhshani

The Aga Khan Award for Architecture focuses on processes of change in parts of the world where the built environment is undergoing rapid transformation, at times with dire consequences. Over the past four decades the Award has sought to understand the nature of this change and to have an impact on design and building in the hope of creating a better quality of life for the people who inhabit these environments. To this end, it recognises exemplary projects and shares the lessons they offer with all those who play a role in this endeavour – architects, planners, government agencies, clients and, above all, the final users of the buildings. Each three-year cycle of the Award involves an exhaustive search for innovative solutions and positive achievements which highlight the significant contribution that architecture can make towards shaping and improving our lives.

From the outset the Award has made both the architectural profession and the wider public aware of a broad new approach to what constitutes architecture. The 15 projects selected in the very first 1977–80 cycle engaged with a wide range of issues, from conservation to slum upgrading, and embraced traditional as well as new designs. Works by both emerging architectural talents and established practices were celebrated alongside the efforts of clients and builders. Together, these projects spoke of the plurality of societies in countries where Muslims have a significant presence, from Indonesia to Morocco.

This pluralistic approach has been pursued by successive independent Master Juries, responding to diverse concerns identified by a rotating Steering Committee for each triennial Award Cycle. The Chairman of the Steering Committee is His Highness the Aga Khan, who established the Award in 1977 to recognise architecture's primary role in improving the quality of life in fast-changing Muslim societies.

One of the most pressing aspects of such change is the movement of peoples far from their homelands. Sometimes forced, sometimes voluntary, this mass migration – from rural to urban areas, or from one country or continent to another – has given traditionally mono-cultural societies a new character shaped by multilayered identities. But it has also posed challenges. How do you create a sense of cohesion in a disparate population? How do you draw new communities into the public sphere, facilitate their engagement with civil society? The Aga Khan Award for Architecture confronts such issues head on, showcasing projects of excellence that address the aspirations of these communities.

The aim of this publication is to share the findings of the 13th Award Cycle, spanning from 2014 to 2016. Among hundreds of nominations the Master Jury reviewed 348 projects from 69 countries and shortlisted 19 of these for in-depth inspection and expert review. From this shortlist six projects were then selected to share the prize money of 1,000,000 USD. Both the Award recipients and the shortlisted projects propose creative solutions to some of the most relevant issues facing architecture today. While differing in scale and approach, all the projects are part of their contexts and enhance the sense of belonging in their communities. Mohsen Mostafavi sets the tone of this cycle in his introductory piece emphasising architecture, place and plurality, while texts by members of the Master Jury, Steering Committee and on-site review teams eloquently elaborate on key aspects of the projects and the issues raised during their deliberations.

What emerges from the many nominations received, and most notably from the 19 projects featured in this publication, is a sense of what can be achieved when architects and clients work collaboratively, combining their forces in a conscious effort to improve the built environment and the everyday lives of people.

Architecture and Plurality

Mohsen Mostafavi

This cycle of the Aga Khan Award for Architecture, like its predecessors, considered a large and diverse group of built projects from across the globe. One caveat for this Award is that the nominated projects be open to the possibility of use by Muslim communities – a very broad and consequently generous criterion. It is of course also understood that the nominated projects must exhibit a degree of excellence, and in so doing make a contribution to the discipline of architecture and to the field of design more generally.

The first criterion – that of possible use by Muslim communities – decouples the projects from the limits of any specific geography, such as the Middle East. Rather, nominations are sought not only from countries whose population is primarily Muslim but also from other locations where the community of Muslims might be in the minority. The Award's embrace of a wide geography is a recognition of both the reality and the diversity of the types of Muslim communities that exist around the world today.

The second and no less crucial assumption by the Award – that of excellence – acknowledges the value of buildings, landscapes and all manner of civic structures intended to improve the built environment and the quality of people's lives, culturally, socially, aesthetically. In that sense the selected projects are viewed as gifts for their respective users and societies. And in the case of projects from non-Muslim countries this definition extends to the broader community, and not just to Muslims.

The ethos of the Award has always relied on the connections between architecture and pluralism. Architects design buildings that in the best cases are exemplars of a particular type, but ideally they also transcend their formal and typological limits through their engagement with specific programmatic and situational conditions. This tension suggests that the premiated projects, rather than being simply building types imported onto a site, are much more the outcome of a set of negotiations which oscillate between needs/programme, location/geography, conditions/themes and architecture/construction.

The fluid nature of these negotiations suggests that architectural projects increasingly have to respond to situations that require alternative creative solutions. Among other things, this has led to the production of hybrid designs. In this cycle, for example, the Tabiat Pedestrian Bridge in Iran serves both as a bridge – a link between two places – and as a public space of recreation. Similarly, Ceuta Public Library is a place of learning as well as the container of an important archaeological site. In addition to responding to needs and contingencies in a multitude of ways, where possible, the projects also cater for a plurality of users. Through this process, architecture gains the capacity to instigate plurality both as a typological and as a social act.

This is not to claim that all the shortlisted works or Award recipients are concerned with pluralism, but inasmuch as the Award recognises the value of societal engagement through design it also acknowledges the capacity of certain projects to promote plurality. The Micro Yuan'er, one of this cycle's Award recipients, demonstrates this point. The project is located in a central part of Beijing, adjacent to a number of buildings, including a mosque, which serve the Muslim community. Here the traditional courtyard residence, with its mostly elderly inhabitants, has been the subject of conservation and adaptive reuse. A series of carefully designed small structures primarily intended for use by children has been constructed with the aim of enhancing the social life of the building.

This project demonstrates architecture's capacity to juxtapose multiple functions – sometimes known as cross-programming – to provide a setting for bringing together a diversity of unexpected users. In the case of the Micro Yuan'er, this means not just the interaction of both old and young users of the building but also, more implicitly, its use by the neighbourhood's Muslim community.

Just as relevant as the project's social and cultural potentials are its architectural implications. The sensitive additions and modifications to the courtyard suggest how the relationship of architecture to its past could be reimagined in different ways. Instead of turning the original building into a reconstructed museum or a pristine example of preservation, the designers have invested it with new life by considering a scenario that has made it more relevant to the local community – both young and old.

The intimacy of the interior courtyard of the Micro Yuan'er, as a place for the activities of a diversity of people, can be considered alongside the scale of another of this cycle's Award recipients, the Superkilen, a public space project in Denmark. The issue of pluralism has different dimensions here. Whereas in Beijing the contrast between the users is more noticeably acute in terms of age, the Superkilen is located in a part of Copenhagen where many migrants have settled. Consequently, by embracing cultural difference, even if on a modest scale, the public space of the project becomes a site that welcomes people of many ethnicities and national origins. In this case, it is specifically the diversity of the types of exterior space and their treatment which creates a place that can be enjoyed and shared by all.

The design of the Superkilen, by imbuing the space with a sense of delight, provides a setting in which cultural differences can be 'acted out' and yet shared by diverse communities. The particular characteristics of the space have helped also to attract a younger generation of inhabitants to the neighbourhood. Of course the popularity of such projects brings potential benefits – such as reducing the possibility of these areas becoming primarily immigrant neighbourhoods – but it can also lead to gentrification, creating the risk of driving out the very people for whom these public spaces are seen to be a healing environment.

It is by now recognised that the spaces of pluralism also need to encompass potential spaces of conflict or disagreement. Pluralism, or plurality, is not limited to envisioning democracy as a condition of equilibrium amongst the different sectors of society. In the Micro Yuan'er project it is possible to imagine a space of pure happiness between the older occupants of the building and the young users of the library inserted into the middle of the courtyard. But the library is on one level as much an imposition – a change in the practised norms of the courtyard – as it is a reminder of one's own youth and the simple pleasures of play.

Similarly, the Superkilen project brings into stark contrast the juxtaposition of people of different backgrounds, habits and looks, and 'stages' their difference as a means of seeking commonality and friendship. But we should not be naïve, nor overly optimistic, about the outcome of this encounter.

In an unusual and perhaps unexpected turn of events, this cycle of the Award includes two projects from Bangladesh: one a mosque for a community on the outskirts of Dhaka, the other a friendship centre in rural Gaibandha. Both these projects appear to be exemplary responses to their respective programmes. And while appearing to be very different in character, both also use the concept of interiority as the major organising concept and condition of their programme.

In the case of the Bait ur Rouf Mosque it is the interior that provides the atmosphere – the interplay of light and shade – most conducive to prayer and reflection. Similarly, in the Friendship Centre, it is the sunken spaces that provide the spaces of collective gathering that exemplify the aspirations of the building – though here the affect of interiority is in reality produced by the outdoor spaces that are defined by the walls of the adjacent enclosed rooms. This affect is further enhanced by the sunken datum of the building in relation to the landscape of the surrounding agricultural territory. In both these projects it is the sense of interiority that provides the welcoming atmosphere which is a necessary precondition of spaces of plurality. The mosque is the place where a diversity of individuals can come together for prayer.

There is of course an irony to all this, since under the current customs of this mosque women are not allowed to pray within the same building, and therefore even the architect herself is excluded from participation. Nevertheless the architecture of the mosque possesses the capacity for her and others like her to attend. And hopefully this will happen in the near future.

There is another aspect of these two projects that demonstrates their connections to pluralism, and that is the lineage of their architecture. It is clear that the brick architecture of these buildings pays homage to the work in Dhaka of the American architect Louis Kahn. Kahn's architecture, in its simplicity and its focus on the use of a single material, was able to construct a form of order and monumentality that still resonates with the local community. Part of its success is perhaps due to its resistance to image-making and its reliance on the tactile and affective qualities of architecture.

Both Le Corbusier and Kahn, building in India and Bangladesh respectively, tried to reduce the need for highly skilled labour by minimising the complexities of construction. This condition is in contrast to another Award recipient – the Issam Fares Institute of the American University in Beirut, by Zaha Hadid Architects – which explores highly sophisticated means of engineering and construction to produce a building that would be seen as a construction challenge in any part of the globe. At once singular and yet contextual, the institute fits within the overall structure of the campus and helps frame one side of an open public space. The cantilevered upper floors of the tilted building establish a visual link with the landscape beyond the courtyard. In turn this connection with the landscape is accentuated by the sinuous ramp that provides access to the upper-level entrance, creating along the way a dramatic viewing platform for the visitor. The ramp also further enhances the liminal character of the building, in terms of its siting.

The elegance and sophistication of this building and the quality of its construction are not common features in contemporary architecture. Such an aspirational project clearly also required an inspiring client who was willing to take a risk. This and other Award recipients and shortlisted projects demonstrate the mission of the Aga Khan Award in pursuit of excellence in architecture, regardless of scale and budget – as evidenced by the modest budget of some of the projects shown in this publication.

To help us grasp their primary thematic references and contributions, the Award recipients and shortlisted projects have been placed under a variety of different headings, such as Community, Conservation and Construction. While these headings only partially define the character of a work, and many of the projects obviously share multiple themes, it remains important for the reader to consider small clusters of topical affiliations amongst the projects, as a way of understanding and witnessing the state of architectural investigation within a specific area.

The selection of the projects presented in this book has been the subject of a rigorous process established by His Highness the Aga Khan and overseen by the Award secretariat. This process includes the roles of the Steering Committee and the Jury as well as the On-Site Reviewers, who ensure that Award recipients have also been subject to expert post-occupancy investigation.

The commitment to design as an agent of change and as a direct means of improving the quality of life of the users of buildings and landscapes is the significant mandate of the Award. It is true, therefore, that the Award has a social and cultural perspective, but it is equally true that the Award sees architecture as the primary means of achieving its social and plural aspirations.

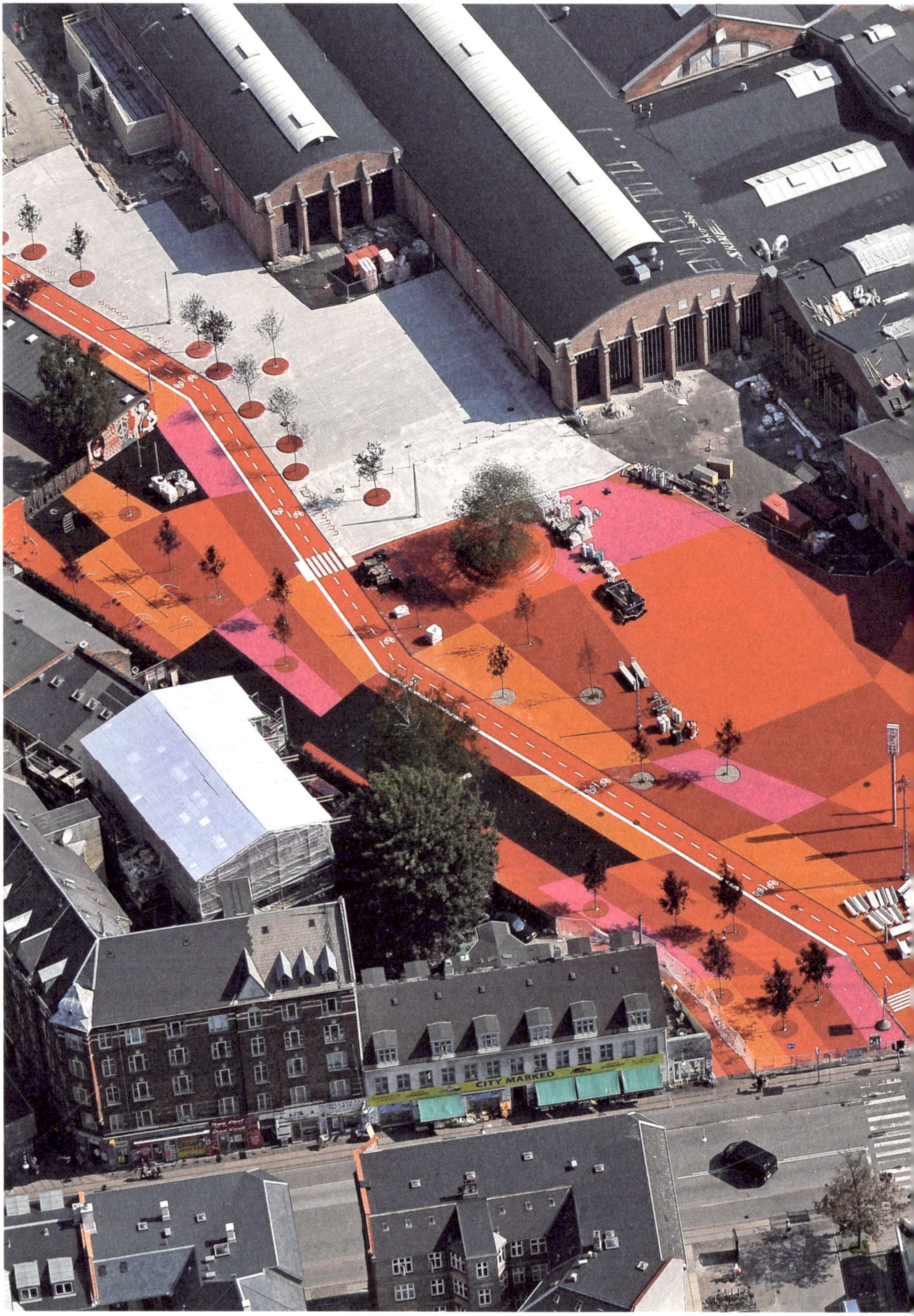
CITY MARKED

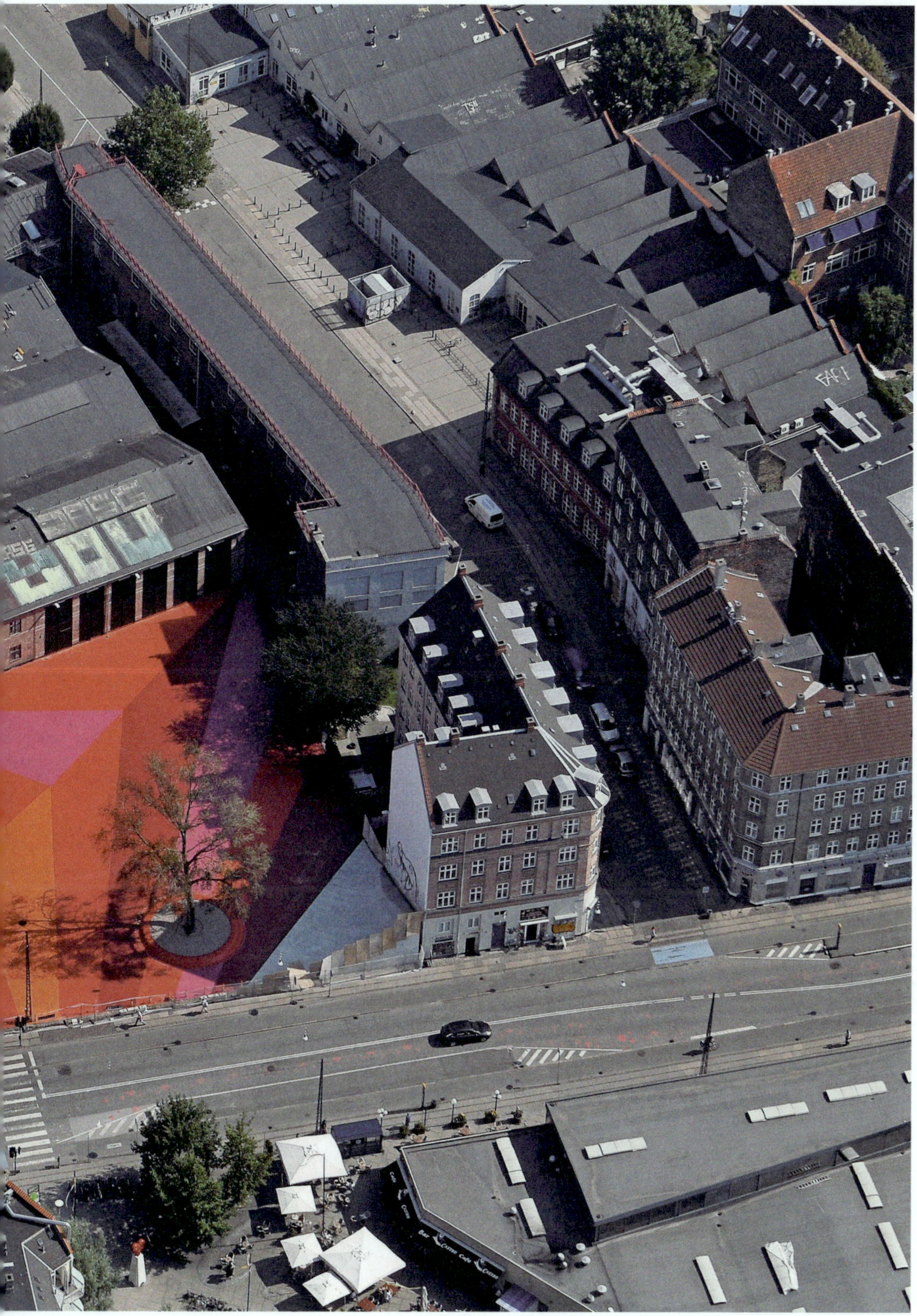

Bait ur Rouf Mosque, Dhaka, Bangladesh

LG
الجی
LG K10
سبک خود را انتخاب کنید

Spaces for Diversity: A Plea for Pluralism

Luis Fernández-Galiano

Architecture can build pluralism. In a world shattered by the tension between globalisation and nationalism, the built environment can provide stages for this conflict to be choreographed, bridging the gap between the cosmopolitan and the local through dialogue and compromise. The impact of mass migration has altered the social and political landscape of many western democracies, from the US to the UK, where the Brexit vote has been the most dramatic expression of the widespread unease that is menacing the European Union's institutional cohesion. Identity-based nationalism is on the rise, and plurality is increasingly perceived as a risk rather than as a richness. But political pluralism is the only hope of survival in this sea of troubles, and its privileged scenario is the *polis,* where top-down policies and bottom-up participation converge. Winston Churchill wrote that 'we shape our buildings; thereafter they shape us', and the same could be said of the spaces of the city, which ultimately shape the forms of our communities, their design favouring or hindering the interaction between cultural or ethnic groups. So architecture can build pluralism, providing plural spaces – places that promote diversity and create a common ground for our living together.

The Aga Khan Award for Architecture has celebrated these spaces for pluralism in the past, and in fact its very structure is designed to bring into dialogue a plurality of approaches springing from very diverse geographic or cultural backgrounds. Far from exclusively recognising major works from major architects – as most other architectural prizes do – the Award has brought together skyscrapers and mud huts, heritage and innovation, workspaces and museums, urban plans and tiny constructions, iconic buildings by prestigious offices and humble achievements by anonymous craftsmen. This phenomenal variety is further reinforced by the credit given to the many different actors who bring architecture into being: architects, to be sure, but also clients, builders, craftsmen and even the members of the community who take care of the running and maintenance of the building, promoting a perception of the environment as a collective endeavour where a plurality of interests and voices must be joined in an articulated conversation for the project to succeed. Pluralism, then, is inscribed in the spirit and the protocols of the Award, and the extraordinary variety of the works selected in this cycle eloquently expresses this commitment, exhibiting a remarkable consistency with the goals pursued in previous editions in its already long history.

Beyond the pluralism of the Award itself, there are always some projects that manage to embody plurality in an exemplary manner, and this is the case –

in the current 13th cycle – with Copenhagen's Superkilen, an urban park in a culturally diverse, socially fraught district of Denmark's capital city. As is well known, the country is so admired worldwide that many consider it a social and political model worthy of emulation. Francis Fukuyama, in *The Origins of Political Order,* goes as far as proposing 'getting to Denmark' as the challenge that most democracies face today, perceiving the Scandinavian country as a particularly successful institutional arrangement that should serve as a beacon for others. However, of late, the lack of integration of different immigrant cultures has created significant tensions in Danish society, made worse, since the cartoon controversy in 2005, by widespread Muslim unrest and the unhappy rise of xenophobic, populist movements. In this context, the completion of Superkilen through the combined efforts of the architects of BIG – Bjarke Ingels Group, the landscape designers Topotek 1 and the artist group Superflex is a colossal achievement because it faces the current dilemmas of immigration-shocked European societies head on – with stupendous imagination and user participation – and finds an answer in pluralism.

At this point we should probably point out that pluralism and multiculturalism are not interchangeable terms. Multiculturalism has a bad press these days, after the failure in many contexts to sustain an archipelago of different cultures coexisting as self-sufficient islands. The German chancellor Angela Merkel – so courageous and generous in her attitude towards immigration – did not hesitate to recognise that what many call 'multikulti' has not really worked. But the reaction to this failure need not be the imposition of a single culture in each country – the preferred defence of nationalist, jingoist movements. On the contrary, the cultural diversity of immigrants can be understood as a richness that can flourish under a pluralist system that does not isolate different backgrounds and experiences in ethnic enclosures but rather allows cultures to cross-fertilise through contact and conversation, recognising the relativity of each worldview and resolving conflicts with the tools of dialogue and trust. This is exactly what the Superkilen project has been able to achieve, transforming a once dangerous neighbourhood into a cross between an amusement park and a world's fair of urban objects curated by the residents – a cherished space for the plural communities on both sides of the *kilen,* the wedge, as well as a new tourist destination in the city.

Not immune to the deep xenophobic, anti-immigration currents that are slowly eroding the foundations of the European Union, Denmark too is now sadly tarnished by Islamophobia – brought violently to the surface here with the anti-mosque campaigns of the Danish People's Party. Against this hostility, Copenhagen's Superkilen is a phenomenal antidote, creating public space for diverse identities, highlighting plurality and addressing political conflicts and social controversies with the weapons of bold creativity, daring humour and participatory design, thus knitting a web of emotional connections that create a sense of belonging, empowering the community and endowing everyone involved with a feeling of pride. If architecture can breed pluralism, surely this is a fine example that should inspire others. The aesthetic imagination and social awareness shown by Superkilen is a tribute to the architects and artists who designed it with the residents, and also to the clients, the City of Copenhagen and the philanthropic association RealDania. And the extraordinary success of the project is living proof that pluralism in the built environment can and should be a guiding thread in the labyrinthine paths that are opening up ahead of us in these troubled times.

Pluralism: Engaging Difference in an Interdependent World

Diana L Eck

The plurality of peoples and cultures has come to characterise every part of the world today. No longer can maps be colour-coded to indicate the population of each major continent and sector. In fact, every part of the world is swirling with the colours and textures of the whole. Communications and migration have brought disparate cultures and energies into constant proximity and contact. Living with diversity and difference – creatively, sympathetically and wisely – is the challenge of the decades ahead.

The world of the twenty-first century has been transformed in almost unimaginable ways by the currents of globalisation, communications and migration. The satellite and fibre-optic technologies that span the continents and the oceans have brought the world closer – the global world, the immediate world of our own society, the local worlds we call home. Powerful communications networks create worldwide markets, deploy worldwide advertising strategies and become worldwide news-brokers. Brazilian soap operas are seen in Turkey, American sitcoms in South India. Headlines from South Africa, cricket scores from Karachi and breaking news from Iran pop up on the smartphones nestled in our pockets.

Banking, commerce, manufacturing and transportation create global networks, connected and interconnected. For better or for worse, OshKosh B'gosh stores for children's clothing can be found in glitzy malls in Kuala Lumpur; Kentucky Fried Chicken and Dunkin' Donuts in the streets of Yogyakarta. Taj Hotels provide refuge and luxury worldwide and Mahindra tractors are the best-selling tractors everywhere. American architectural firms contract for design projects in China and India, while Indian call centres process travel reservations for Americans. Consumers and manufacturers are interconnected and inextricably interdependent.

Along with the revolutions in communications and commerce, the mass movement of peoples as economic migrants and refugees has transformed societies the world over. In the United States, the 1965 Immigration and Nationalities Act opened the door to immigrants from Asia who had long been subject to harsh exclusion policies. In addition to the many new post-1965 immigrants from India and China, refugees have settled in America from war-torn countries in Southeast Asia, the Middle East and Africa. All this has infused American cities and towns with a fresh mix of peoples, and a more complex cultural, religious and architectural landscape has emerged. Alongside the churches there are now thousands of mosques, temples and gurdwaras, many transformed from other uses, but increasingly purpose-built and designed as new landmarks.

In Europe, formerly homogeneous European societies find themselves challenged – and perplexed – by a new and unaccustomed diversity. There are Hindu temples in Bern and Strasbourg, landmark mosques and Islamic centres in Lyon and London, and debates about the minaret in Switzerland. Nations that have imagined their community along more unitary lines are today factually multifaith and multicultural. But holding together cultural, ethnic, religious difference under a shared political roof is no small task. What does it mean to be Swedish? To be French or British? Who decides? What does it mean to be a citizen in the context of a society in which one's co-citizens may not share one's own deeply held values or cultural traditions? What does it mean to give positive expression to diversity – in the arts and in education, in architecture and in the urban landscape?

The process of globalisation has meant the marbling of cultures and communities in new ways. Even as people wrestle with the contentious issues of diversity, they are often brought together by the energies of popular culture and food. Bollywood and bhangra, tai-chi and yoga, salsa and burritos, chicken tikka masala and naan, halal and kosher have all become standard in the cultural mix. But while we may eat one another's food and dance one another's dances, we have not boldly addressed the deep differences that divide the world. Our ignorance and prejudice circle the globe along with our credit card numbers and our greenhouse gases. The globalisation of our imagination, our artistic vision, our conscience and consciousness is still underdeveloped. The moral and cultural implications of globalisation are little explored. As nations and peoples, we understand one another too little.

Diversity can and has meant the creation of ghettoes with little traffic between them. It can and has meant the building of fences to ensure that those who are different are kept in their own backyard. It can and has meant the dominance of the majority and the grudging acquiescence of minority communities. It can and has meant open conflict and even war. Diversity is a given, everywhere. But alone, it means nothing. Diversity is only the raw material of cultures that now must develop an ethos of pluralism.

Diversity without real encounters or relationships will yield increasing tensions in our societies. Pluralism, on the other hand, means engagement with the other, a decision not to avoid or avert, but rather to reach out. As His Highness the Aga Khan has put it, 'Pluralism results when people decide to value and understand human differences through mutual respect and civic inclusion.' Unlike diversity, pluralism is not a given; it is a choice and an achievement.

A further definition of pluralism is that it is not just tolerance, but the active seeking of understanding across lines of difference. Though tolerance is perhaps a necessary public virtue, especially considered in the light of intolerance, it does not require us to know anything about one another. It is also a perspective held from a disequilibrium of power: the influential may tolerate what they do not like, while the powerless may tolerate what is dished out to them. Put up with it, but don't investigate further – in pulling down the shades of our vision, mere tolerance cheats us of the experience of astonishment as we discover the daily lives, creative achievements and artistic genius of those we tolerate as the 'other'. And, of course, tolerance is too thin a foundation for the world of difference and proximity we inhabit today. It does nothing to remove our ignorance of one another, to counter our lack of appreciation for each other's aesthetic, literary and architectural traditions. Depriving societies of the genius of our own diversity, mere tolerance simply leaves in place the stereotype, the half-truth, the fears that underlie old patterns of division and violence, with increasingly costly consequences.

For critics, the very word 'pluralism' seems to imply a weak form of relativism, the compromise of one's principles and visions in the search for the lowest common denominator. For some, the very word implies that all worldviews and perspectives are the same. But let us emphasise that pluralism begins with difference, not with sameness, and the paradigm of pluralism does not require us to leave behind our identities, our philosophical or religious views, our cherished particularities and our commitments. No, pluralism is the encounter of commitments, the genuine encounter of who we really are. It means holding our deepest differences, even our religious differences, not in isolation, but in relationship to one another. It may well involve argument over very significant matters: How do we understand our human relation to nature and the environment? How do we envision a complex community, a diverse urban environment? What do we value most in family and community life? What do we see as beautiful and artistically elevating? Pluralism does not reach for the lowest common denominator, but for the highest level of mutual understanding and the appreciation of difference.

Thus pluralism is dependent on dialogue. The language of pluralism is that of give and take, criticism and self-criticism, argument and sometimes apology. Dialogue does not mean everyone will agree with one another. Dialogue means both speaking and listening, a process that reveals both common understandings and real differences. Pluralism involves the commitment to being 'at the table' – with one's commitments and perspectives, and with openness towards the others who are present. The 'table' of which we speak is sometimes a real sit-down-and-talk table, but more often the sites of encounter are to be found in every sector of our society – in our neighbourhoods and malls, schools and universities, hospitals and wellness centres, the workplace and the office, city councils and zoning boards, planning and development projects. These are workshops of pluralism where the language of dialogue is spoken. It is the language of respectful relationship, and pluralism requires of us this kind of relational ethos and sensibility.

His Highness the Aga Khan, the spiritual leader of the Ismaili Muslims, has become one of the great spokesmen for pluralism today. Involved as he is in issues of education, healthcare and development the world over, he sees from experience that the contemporary world absolutely requires the nurturing of pluralist societies. 'It is my conviction', he says, 'that strengthening institutions that support pluralism is as critical for the welfare and progress of human society as are alleviating poverty and preventing conflict. In fact, all three are intimately related.' Yet at a time when the interdependence of societies is a clear and salient fact of global order, we still hear the strident voices of those who insist upon singular social identities and the dominance of majorities. As the Aga Khan puts it, 'The rejection of pluralism is pervasive across the globe, and this rejection plays a significant role in breeding destructive conflicts.'

Pluralist societies do not just happen by themselves. Rather, they are, as the Aga Khan has noted, 'products of enlightened education and continuous investment by governments and all of civil society in recognising and celebrating the diversity of the world's peoples'. For people in all walks of life, investing in a future in which diversity is not divisive means imagining and designing institutions, public and private, that are inclusive and give expression to an ethos of respect for diversity of people and communities.

The Centre for Pluralism, launched by the Aga Khan and located in Ottawa, has given a rationale for developing a culture of inclusion:
– When valued rather than feared, human diversity enriches and benefits a society.

- Having difference recognised by the state and the nation fosters belonging, participation and equality.
- Cultures of inclusion do not erase difference or disagreement; rather, they offer ways to manage conflict peacefully.
- Majority identities and minority aspirations must be considered.
- Pluralist societies require ongoing work and investment – by citizens, civil societies and governments – but the returns are enormous.

The American sociologist Richard Florida writes of what he calls the 'diversity advantage' of cities. Diverse cities are more likely to attract a 'creative class' of people – themselves cosmopolitan, inventive and artistic – who are more likely to thrive in a culture of complexity, difference, exchange and cooperation. Studying old cosmopolitan cities as well as the multicultural cities of today, Florida sees a positive correlation between a city's success and the appreciation of diversity. In his study, *The Rise of the Creative Class,* he draws an explicit correlation between economic development and a welcoming cultural climate that crosses boundaries and attracts creative talent.

The city is what the sociologist Lewis Mumford called 'energy converted into culture'. Today, great world-cities like New York, London, Mumbai or Shanghai and countless smaller cities the world over are swirling with the energies of their diversity. These are the workshops of pluralism, where visionary leadership is challenged to create the human and physical infrastructure of relationship – the civic networks, the bridges, the housing blocks and the institutions of education and the arts. The Aga Khan sums up the challenge:

'Pluralism results when a society actively reorients its political, social, economic and educational systems to recognise and secure the equality of every person as a citizen. Pluralism does not erase human differences. A commitment to pluralism redefines diversity as a collective source of common good. When valued and enabled through the practices of pluralism, diversity is a foundation for civic cohesion.'

What is Pluralism? Some Philosophical and Historical Reflections

Akeel Bilgrami

Some Philosophical Distinctions

Pluralism would be beside the point in a time or place – if such a time or place ever existed – when societies did not consist of plural points of view, when there was uniformity of opinion on all important matters, in a word, when there was a cultural homogeneity. But in the modern period plural points of view are present in virtually all societies we know of, generated initially by conquest or migration from *outside* a society and later often due to increasing consciousness of new forms of identity emerging from *within* a society such as, to take just one relatively recent example, gender identity in the last half-century or more.

Pluralism, however, is not to be conflated with the *fact* of such plurality of cultures in a society. It is a *normative* doctrine, an *ideal* not a fact. It is an ideal of *respect* relevant in societies that contain plural cultures and points of view.

How shall we understand the special kind of respect that defines the pluralist ideal?

Each person knows someone (perhaps many others) whom she recognises to be as wise and good and knowledgeable as she is, but with whom she deeply differs on one or other matter of importance whether it be moral or religious or political. Despite the depth of difference, however, she may have great respect for his (their) wisdom, goodness, and knowledge and therefore, in turn, for the point of view with which she differs. Respect of this kind can define not just such relations between individual persons but relations between whole cultures. When it does so, it is properly called 'pluralism'.

So understood, as a form of respect, the ideal of pluralism is to be distinguished from the liberal ideal of toleration. The very term 'toleration' suggests that one is putting up with something for which one might not have any respect. If toleration entails respect it is only of a very abstract kind – respect for a citizen's autonomy to hold whatever views she wishes, even if one does not specifically respect her for her views. Pluralism, by contrast, respects difference, not merely the autonomy of citizens to be different.

At the same time, as a doctrine about cultural difference, pluralism is to be distinguished along different lines from cultural *relativism*. Relativism holds that there are values that are true (or false) only relative to particular cultures and so such truth (or falsity) as they have does not speak at all to other cultures. They are incommensurate with the values of other cultures. One culture may recognise that another culture adheres to certain values but that recognition is purely detached and disengaged, it is merely an academic or ethnographic comprehension of another. There is no *engagement* of one culture by another. At best, one can go to another culture and get converted by 'going native', a form of defection rather than transformation via influence or dialogue or persuasion. By contrast, pluralism, despite acknowledging genuine difference between the values of different cultures, does not consider values across cultures to be incommensurate in this way. That is to say, difference does not engender detachment and indifference; rather it leaves it completely open that one may learn from other cultures and seek to influence other cultures, in turn, through mutual engagement.

This distinctness from cultural relativism makes it clear that nothing in pluralism requires one to stamp every commitment of every culture as true or right simply because of the fact that it is avowed by a culture. Respect for cultures does not concede to them that automatic form of self-validation. One may certainly find some values of another culture (as indeed of one's own culture) to be wrong and indeed that is precisely why one, unlike as with relativism, often seeks to engage with that culture – seeking to change its mind and thereby overcome the disagreement over values and practices. So long as such engagement is done with the respect that defines the pluralist ideal, as I have expounded it, pluralism may insist that differing cultures are commensurate and can find each other to be wrong without giving up on the pluralism. So a question then arises: what is it to engage with respect with a culture with which one disagrees and moreover, crucially, to do so with a more specific form of respect than merely the general and abstract form of respect that liberalism grants, the respect for all persons' autonomy and right to an opinion, however false? This is the hard question. Hard because without a good answer to it, we cannot firmly claim to have established what I have insisted on – that pluralism is distinct *both* from liberal toleration *and* from cultural relativism.

The specific form of respect that is the hallmark of pluralism bestows on the engagement with another culture with which one disagrees a very specific quality. The engagement must take the form of attempting to persuade another culture by appealing to some grounds or reasons that are *internal* to the commitments of the *other* culture. That displays a respect for the other culture that goes beyond, that is more specific than, the respect that owes to the abstract recognition of all to have their opinions, however wrong. It respects their substantive moral and psychological economies rather than merely their autonomy and seeks to reason with them within the detail of *their* worldview, taking its particular substantive values seriously and engaging with them so as to persuade it to change its mind or practice on the matter on which there is disagreement. Without such substantive and specific engagement, the pluralist ideal would be indistinguishable from liberal toleration.

It is really because the unique and specific form of respect that defines pluralism allows engagements of this sort – engagements which may result in the overcoming of disagreements and the converging upon certain values and practices – that pluralism often takes a syncretic cultural form where two or more cultures may blend to form common ways of life, even as they remain distinct in genealogical pedigree and leave distinct communities within the society intact. In the realm of religion in particular, syncretic forms of pluralism are far more frequent in popular and folk religiosity than in orthodox and institutionalised religion where such mutual engagement that characterises pluralism is discouraged.

Some Historical Distinctions

Wherever pluralism withers, two starkly opposed cultural attitudes, each in its different way dangerous or repugnant, prevail: one of saying 'You must be my brother!', the other of saying 'You can never be my brother!'. The former is familiar from the religious intolerance of proselytising religions, the latter is familiar from exclusionary forms of hierarchy such as, for instance, the Hindu caste system.

In some ways the former attitude is morally more attractive than the latter because it wishes to share the truth (as it conceives it) with others, thereby showing that it cares enough for others to want them to partake in the truth. But it may often be the more dangerous attitude because it is susceptible to the use of force and violence to enforce the 'must' in 'You must be my brother'.

There are, however, distinctions and points of historical qualification to be observed about this. For centuries the relations between two proselytising religious cultures, Christendom and Islam, were characterised by extreme vilification and violence towards one another both in word and deed. This was partly at least because of the doctrinal proximity of the two religions. Islam posed a threat to Christianity not because it was vastly different – in fact it is hard to imagine such internecine relations between Christianity and Buddhism, say, or Hinduism, which were not only more geographically distant, but remote in concept and outlook. In fact it may be said, with only the merest exaggeration, that the Crusades were fought not because Islam seemed to Christianity to be some wholesale alien worldview to be destroyed, but rather to put down a *heresy* that had emerged in the Arabian lands. The point of immediate relevance, however, is that throughout this period of the Crusades, these two civilisations, for all the violence they perpetrated against each other, learnt from and influenced each other in the sciences, art, literature and philosophy, and they traded with each other in a wide variety of goods. Indeed, Islamic thought and culture often became a hospice for heterodox ideas within Christianity that were threatened with internal persecution. There was, it might be said – perverse as this may sound – health in the hostility. It was the health of contradictory relations that often exist between two robustly equal foes. Pluralism, even a syncretic coalescence, existed in the world of ideas and culture and commerce, while there was a protracted conflict on the military and propaganda battleground. To put it in Huntington's term, this was a genuine *clash* of civilisations, proving that clash – however undesirable in its own terms – is not always incompatible with mutual engagement and the respect that characterises pluralism.

All of this changed with Napoleon's campaigns in Egypt and the British conquest of India, which gave rise to a quite different set of relations between Christendom and Islam, now no longer a conflict between equal sides, but rather defined by feelings of superiority and condescension on the one side and felt to be so by the other, breeding resentment and alienation and dehumanisation rather than a robust sense of conflict. Huntington was not talking of the period of the Crusades so much as this modern period. He was thus really insidiously passing off a *conquest* as a *clash*. There is real significance in this distinction. Pluralism as I have defined it is almost entirely missing in the 'clash' of civilisations of our time, proving that pluralism is only compatible with a clash, that is to say with hostility, even violence, so long as the hostility and violence does not take the form of conquests that define the colonialism of the modern period down to the indirect imperialisms of our own day. Huntington's omnibus term 'clash' glosses over this distinction and the history within which pluralism first flourished and then withered.

A further good question to ask is how the concept of 'pluralism' relates to the recent currency of the term 'multiculturalism'. There is no answering this question without looking again to history, in particular to the political history of European modernity and its evolving doctrines in the passage from pluralism, through nationalism and secularism, to multiculturalism.

In the seventeenth century, power, which was hitherto relatively scattered, first began to be integrated in increasingly centralised states and, as a result of ideas that had emerged with the new science, it was thought that this state power could no longer rest on a legitimacy that appealed to the *divine right* of the monarch who personified the state. It now required a quite different justification and this was sought no longer in theology but in political psychology. What do I mean by psychology? A *feeling* had to be created in the populace. But it was not a feeling directly for the state. It was rather to be a feeling for a new kind of entity that had emerged around then, after the Westphalian peace, an entity with which the state was indissolubly *fused*. Later this fusion would come to be described with a hyphen: the nation-state. The idea was to create a feeling for the first half of the hyphenated conjunction, which because it was inseparable from the second half (an inseparability expressed by the hyphen) would legitimise the state and its exercise of power over the territory that was the 'nation'. 'Nationalism' was subsequently the term used to describe this feeling, this political psychology.

In many parts of the main belt of Europe such a feeling was generated by a standard ploy: by identifying an 'external' enemy *within* the territory (the Jews, the Irish, the Catholics in Protestant countries, the Protestants in Catholic countries...) and despising it and subjugating it as the 'Other', declaring that the nation was 'ours' not theirs. Later, when numerical and statistical forms of discourse were introduced in the study of politics, such categories as majorities and minorities were introduced and this ploy would be called 'majoritarianism'. And so it was that these European nation-building exercises destroyed the relatively unselfconscious pluralism that prevailed prior to modern nationalism, creating entrenched divisions – and often the basis of the majoritarianism was religious. Naturally, there were (often violent) religious minoritarian backlashes against this form of majoritarian nationalism, and the damage done by the civil strife that followed gave rise to the conviction that *religion itself* was responsible for the damage and the damage could only be repaired if religion was kept out of the orbit of the polity. And thus, a new doctrine called 'secularism' emerged – basically to *correct* the politically divisive fallout of these nationalisms – and was extensively consolidated as the frameworking form of governance of the European modern state.

It was only in the last quarter of the twentieth century that it began to be felt that this entrenched secularism was insufficient as a political framework. In the decades after 1945, European economies were reconstructing their war-torn economies that had suffered serious loss of manpower during the war. To deal with this, they permitted large-scale immigration from erstwhile colonies for the first time, more often than not to do the most menial forms of labour. Over the next decades these migrant populations grew to be substantial minorities, often alienated in their new setting, coping with racialist attitudes that they faced with uneasy assimilation and, as a result, they frequently turned to their own religions as a source of dignity and autonomy. Ironically, secularism, which, as the narrative above makes clear, was introduced to repair a damage that had started first with religious majoritarianism, seemed to them quite inadequate as a way of addressing their feelings of helplessness as dislocated minorities. Secularism, because it opposes both religious majorities and minorities, did not speak concessively enough to them *as minorities* with their own religion and culture. It came off as secular majoritarianism, an improvement perhaps on religious majoritarianism, but irrelevant to their predicament. It was to address this dissatisfaction with secularism that the ideal of multiculturalism was formulated, essentially a post-migratory phenomenon in Europe and other countries with increasing immigrant populations, such as Canada and Australia. Multiculturalism, unlike secularism, was intended not simply to lay down the law with indifference to majorities and minorities; it would treat *all* cultures as *minorities,* acknowledging each of their customs and their protocols for living and local self-governance.

What this potted intellectual and social history reveals is that 'multiculturalism' is a selfconscious revivalist version of a pluralism that was a widely pervasive and unselfconscious phenomenon prior to its being undermined by nationalisms based on majoritarianism and the secularism that was brought in later to repair that. Multiculturalism restores pluralism in a more explicitly articulated ideal because the initial pluralist ideal could not be taken for granted in the centuries-long trajectory that followed upon the rise of modern nations along with the political psychology on which they were based. And to this day multiculturalism, our own contemporary selfconscious version of an earlier pluralism, is constantly harassed not only by the sinister right-wing majoritarian nationalisms that have resurfaced but also to some extent by liberal secularists who resent the pressures put on their abstract universalist claims about citizenship by the particularist demands of diversity coming from minorities after a half-century of migrations.

Pluralism: Science and Culture

I have restricted my remarks so far to issues of culture and values. It is frequently thought that plural*ity* is much more prevalent and, therefore, plural*ism* is much more relevant in the realm of culture and value rather than in the realm of science. On the face of it, this is true, but one should proceed with caution in making the distinction too starkly binary.

On the face of it, one thinks this: science formulates laws that govern all of the phenomena that science studies – whether they be in Manhattan or the Malabar – and so there cannot be the kind of difference we find in the phenomena that we study when we study culture.

But now consider the science of medicine.

Ever since the development of modern medicine in Europe, there has been some accomplished sneering, dismissive of older traditions in more distant lands, whether Ayurveda or Unani or traditional Chinese medicine ... denying their claims to effective treatment of a variety of afflictions. But in more recent years, there has been a slow and somewhat grudging recognition, even among the established institutions of medical *science,* of the success of a variety of treatments in a range of indigenous traditions. This in itself does nothing to undermine the modernist outlook of science. The outlook does not need to deny the empirical facts about the efficacies of traditional medicine, but what it needs to insist on rather is this: the efficacies of *both* traditional medicine and modern 'allopathic' medicine are to be accounted for by a *common underlying* explanatory theoretical framework of science. Such an explanation would retain the universality of scope that – as I said, on the face of it – is uniquely demanded of science but is missing in culture.

But this point may be convincing only because we are looking in the wrong place for plurality in the matter of medicine. The plurality does not lie most deeply in the fact of there being relatively effective medical traditions outside of western modernity, it does not consist in baldly and simply denying that the curative success of both modern and traditional medicine must be explained by the same underlying physical theory; it consists rather in denying this latter claim by making a *prior* claim: that there is a plurality of conceptions of *the very idea of success,* of what counts as cure.

Many traditional cultures simply do not see the body as a self-standing target of treatment. For them, the body is shot through with meaning and value and emotions, it is never merely the body, never merely a physical thing. Thus medical cure is not just a repair of physical functions and health, it is a restoration just as much of meaning and emotional equilibrium. To think that one simply treats a tooth or an organ as a physical thing by a pill or surgery is to miss the entire point about what a body is or what health itself is. And it won't even do to say that one can cure the body first with a pill or with surgery and that then *causes* a restoration of emotional equilibrium. It is not a causal relation between body and the more rarified phenomena of meaning and emotions. The body, as I put it above, *is itself* shot through with meaning and emotions. So it is not a causal *conjunction* of body and something loftier. There is no separability of the two. And so the plurality lies in there being entirely different conceptions of what a body is: modern medicine simply has a different idea of the body and therefore of health. Hence, to insist that there is a common underlying scientific theory that explains the efficacies of modern and traditional medicine literally makes no sense because these systems of medicine are seeking different efficacies. There is no common phenomenon to be explained by a single underlying theory. That is where the plurality lies.

To deny this would be to refuse the idea that there are different conceptions of the body, to refuse the body as conceived in broader terms than the merely physical, as possessed of meaning, say, and properties of feeling and emotion. To draw an analogy with theatre, that would be like seeing a stage prop – a table on a stage, say – as merely a swarm of molecules, with none of the meaning that it has in the performance of the play, as a site of conviviality, perhaps, or of tense family negotiation. That would be to fail to understand the nature of theatre and similarly, by the lights of tradition, modern medicine fails to understand the nature of health and of cure.

A genuine pluralism would recognise, then, that modern science and traditional medicine have different conceptions of health itself, not just different efficacious paths to a commonly understood notion of health which can then be given a common underlying explanation in science.

The relevance of this to architecture should perhaps now be obvious. Like the body, it is not as if a building is two different things (a physical construction and a contextually *meaningful* percept) that can be the targets of separate understandings. It is *one* thing, there is no physical building that is not shot through with meaning. From the point of view of the architect, engineering itself is a cultural discipline.

Place and Plurality

Azim Nanji

The 2014 Nobel Prize in Medicine recognised an important finding by two neuroscientists, namely their discovery of 'how we know where we are in space'. In identifying the critical role of 'place cells' – our own inner GPS – the scientists illuminated how we position ourselves in the world and how we navigate our way through the complexities of our environment.

These neurobiological insights indicate not only how we engage with our natural and built environment, but also, more crucially, how our innate sense of place is a kind of compass intertwining aspects of culture, identity, memory and well-being.

In view of our current state of knowledge, it is too early to speculate about the specific relevance these findings might have for architecture. Nevertheless, we have now been given an evidence-based lens through which to grasp the multidimensional nature of our total environment and the need for deep intelligence in addressing its complexities. This understanding encourages us to value plurality and diversity as inescapable facts and to resist the drive to homogenise and normalise the ways in which we create place.

Through its history and its evolving intent, the Award has shown us why it is so important to recover this relationship between our sense of place and the plurality of experience – here specifically the experience, past and present, of Muslim societies and communities, wherever they are in the world. In the jury citation for the 2016 Pritzker Architecture Prize, awarded to the Chilean architect, Alejandro Aravena, we find an echo and reinforcement of this same appreciation for 'a new generation of architects that has a holistic understanding of the built environment and has clearly demonstrated the ability to connect social responsibility, economic demands, design of human habitat and the city.'

The multiplicity of economies and cultures in our times threatens to create a disequilibrium that sets the local and the global on a collision path. Perhaps the task of 'building' can offer narratives that sustain the hope of creating a better future in the spirit of pluralism.

Steering Committee Brief

For almost 40 years, the Aga Khan Award for Architecture has worked on expanding the horizons of the practice of architecture throughout Muslim societies to address a variety of challenges. In doing so, the Award has promoted successful interventions in the built environment that have contributed to social and economic development and to empowering communities. In all instances, the Award has adhered to the highest standards of architectural practice, while recognising diverse innovative approaches that challenge and expand conventional boundaries, whether technical, professional or conceptual.

The Award has an open and inclusive perspective that engages with projects contributing to transforming the quality of life for Muslim communities in various settings, whether rural or urban, national or diasporic. The Muslim *Umma* is diverse and pluralistic in its values and aspirations. In a world where cultural expressions are increasingly challenged by globalising commercial, political and social forces on the one hand, and by rising trends that promote national and religious exclusivity on the other, Muslim communities worldwide need to engage in a continuous re-examination of issues relating to identity. The Award aims to help identify positive modes that enable established Muslim communities to take on the challenges of globalisation; to empower emerging Muslim communities to positively negotiate their role within the multicultural contexts of their host countries; and to extend the outreach of Muslim cultures into the world at large by promoting understanding and openness.

We also need to keep in mind that parts of the Islamic world are suffering high levels of political instability and violence that often are related to contested conceptions of the social and cultural roles of Islam. This instability and violence has often spilled over to affect areas outside the traditional boundaries of the Islamic world. These conditions make it ever more pressing to emphasise agencies of openness, pluralism and tolerance within Muslim communities. This is a role that the Award has taken on since its inception, and that role is more relevant and pressing than ever.

The Award should continue to address ongoing economic and social transformations in the Islamic world as that world becomes more heavily engaged in transnational production and consumption networks. The impact of this development on local communities has been enormous, with social changes often lagging behind economic development. In the review process, issues of equity, sustainability, political participation and good governance therefore should be considered as they are at the root of developments affecting the built environment.

The Award has also strived to extend its explorations to new frontiers. It has acknowledged buildings that address environmental and climatic challenges, has engaged with issues affecting the urban scale, and has acknowledged the role of various agents in forming the built environment. These agents include not only architects, planners and other related professionals, but also a wide diversity of clients and other stakeholders such as governmental bodies, civil society institutions and local communities. New approaches for addressing the challenges of urbanism have also been explored, ranging from the use of reforestation at the edges of growing cities, to initiatives in urban planning and preservation that develop confidence and trust between conflicting stakeholders. The Master Jury is encouraged to explore still new frontiers for interventions in the built environment.

Moreover, Muslim communities throughout the world are facing mounting challenges relating to the quality of their built environments, which makes the continuous re-examination and redefinition of the issues that the Award emphasises an ongoing priority. Environmental and ecological concerns are becoming increasingly critical as levels of air, water and soil pollution grow, and also as challenges resulting from climate change and scarcity of water resources reach grave proportions. Many urban centres are undergoing serious and continuous deterioration as a result of the mounting pressures of rapidly increasing populations and crumbling infrastructures. This is evident in a multiplicity of urban problems including overcrowding, sprawl and overwhelming levels of traffic congestion. There is a need to identify and acknowledge tools that have successfully enhanced the resilience of the built environment, allowing it to face such challenges.

The Award therefore needs to continue to identify innovative interventions that incorporate new technological and social mechanisms while also recognising responses that fall within traditional realms of architecture. In doing so, the Award acknowledges the importance of developing contextual, integrated and multidisciplinary solutions that contribute to elevating people's well-being and quality of life. These include master planning and other tools for managing urban development, public transportation solutions, the creation and development of various types of public spaces, and infrastructure initiatives serving every scale from small local communities to metropolitan urban populations – all are a high priority for the Award. Industrial sites and places of work also are to be carefully considered with a view to providing architectural excellence as well as securing safe, comfortable and pleasant environments for their users. Another important issue is the long-standing neglect of rural societies, where architectural and planning solutions can greatly contribute to alleviating conditions of distress. While it is unlikely that any individual project can deal with all of the issues we have proposed for your consideration, we hope that the projects identified for premiation by the Master Jury will take a thoughtful and coherent approach, on both the individual and collective levels, to addressing at least some of the threshold criteria identified above.

In conclusion, the Steering Committee recommends that the Master Jury give consideration to projects responding to the following concerns:
- How projects may address the challenges of globalisation, with particular reference to economic and social changes, urbanisation, migrations and diasporas;
- How the principles of pluralism and mutual respect may be embraced and reflected in architectural design;
- How new technological and environmental challenges may be addressed through infrastructures and innovative approaches;
- How the historical environment may be protected, restored and valued for relevant uses and needs;
- How projects may help communities to respond to crises, disasters and conflicts.

The Steering Committee would like to encourage the Master Jury to recognise projects that take risks by placing themselves at the edge of current practice, anticipating trends and responding to unpredictable challenges.

Finally, the Steering Committee recommends that due attention be given to excellence in design, quality of construction and project implementation, at the scale of architecture, landscape, urbanism, private and public space, as well as the appropriate use of human and material resources.

Report of the Master Jury

Tradition and modernity are often seen as opposing forces, locked together in a permanent state of tension. This is perhaps most keenly felt in societies undergoing rapid transformation, where the aspirations of the future confront the lessons of the past in complex and testing ways. Continuity has historically been one of the cornerstones of Islamic societies throughout the world, but the enormous shifts over the past 50 years, whether as a result of war, migration or advances in communication, present new challenges and opportunities for architects and those involved in shaping the built environment. Unique among architecture awards, the Aga Khan Award seeks projects across a vast range of contexts, cultures and conditions. Throughout its history, it has also celebrated works that straddle the sometimes uneasy divide between tradition and modernity.

The jury for the 13th cycle embraced the notion of plurality, exploring not just projects in diverse contexts but the boundaries of the discipline itself, recognising that new knowledge sometimes emerges in the lines between categories. For established practitioners, this posed a particular dilemma: how to identify merit in projects whose very terms force us to question the limits of our understanding. The traditional categories of our discipline – corporate, cutting-edge, infrastructure, socially responsive, environmentally sound – are not as fixed or concrete as they once seemed. How does one push an edge that is continuously shifting? If a woman may never enter a space that she herself has conceived and executed, then can that project be considered 'cutting-edge'? Or if a building blurs the divide between landscape, dwelling and ecology, can it be considered to push the boundaries of all three? Rather than respect the conventional segregation of architecture into works of different scale and scope, the jury sought to paint a more nuanced and perhaps even pixelated portrait of a world – and a discipline – in a state of flux.

The six Award recipients, arrived at after long and sometimes heated discussion, accurately reflect the wide range of entries: a pedestrian bridge that privileges use over form; a sacred space that plays inventively with tradition; a project that is at once landscape and building; a bold, contemporary insertion into a traditional setting; a diminutive library operating at a much larger micro-urban scale; and an urban park that provides new forms of public space.

In such a context, a universal language of architecture no longer seems appropriate: what remains are creative and often modest site-specific responses that generate new vocabularies of their own.

Bait ur Rouf Mosque, Dhaka, Bangladesh
Friendship Centre, Gaibandha, Bangladesh
Micro Yuan'er Children's Library and Art centre, Beijing, China
Superkilen, Copenhagen, Denmark
Tabiat Pedestrian Bridge, Tehran, Iran
Issam Fares Institute, Beirut, Lebanon

Luis Fernández-Galiano (Chair), Suad Amiry, Emre Arolat, Akeel Bilgrami, Hameed Haroon, Lesley Lokko, Mohsen Mostafavi, Dominique Perrault, Hossein Rezai

AWARD RECIPIENTS

COMMUNITY

How can architecture benefit a community? There are many ways in which buildings can enhance the lives of a group of users. They can take many forms, ranging from small-scale libraries located in diverse locations – often in close proximity to schools, but serving the whole neighbourhood – to training facilities that become places of welcome and friendship. Other community buildings might equally well be places of cultural interaction and learning, such as the Thread Cultural Centre in Senegal, or places of entertainment, like the New Power Station in Azerbaijan.

Friendship Centre

Gaibandha, Bangladesh

The centre is a training facility for the NGO Friendship, which works with communities living in the rural flatlands of northern Bangladesh. In this region permanent buildings are conventionally raised 2.4 m off the ground, to mitigate flooding, but the budget did not allow that here. Instead, an earthen embankment was built around the site, with stairs leading down into the building from open ends. Adopting the vocabulary of a walled town, the programme is organised around a series of pavilions that look inwards onto courtyards and reflecting pools. Because of the embankment wall, there is no horizontal light, so in essence the centre is top-lit. This connection, between an architecture of the land and the light coming down from above, makes for a very elemental building.

The plan is cruciform. Circulation runs lengthwise down the centre, connecting the two external stairs, while the two parts of the programme bisect the site in the other direction – the 'Ka' block contains the more public spaces, such as teaching rooms and offices, and the 'Kha' block, the more private accommodation. Between the two blocks are large tanks for collecting rainwater. The landscaping is in two planes – at grade, brick paving in all the circulation areas and courtyards; and above, earthen rooftops with green cover, which act as insulators and absorb the rain.

Traditional brick masonry is used in a modernist idiom. The bricks were sorted for size, shape and colour by the site engineers, who kept only three out of every ten bricks produced by the local kiln. Of these, only the most aesthetically pleasing were used to create the exposed brick finish, while the remainder were incorporated into the foundations and other unseen parts of the building. In parts, the structure is reinforced with concrete, as this is a seismic zone.

Monolithic, a seamless continuity of material in harmony with its surroundings, the Friendship Centre embodies what Louis Kahn described as an 'architecture of the land.'

Citation

Looking at the sunken brick compound of the Friendship Centre, one is reminded of the archaeological remains of the nearby Vasu Bihara Buddhist temple, built during the third and fourth century. The Friendship Centre blurs the boundaries between an archaeological site and an architectural and landscape project. Through its configuration and its use of grassed rooftops it becomes part and parcel of the surrounding landscape. This grounding is both literal and metaphorical. The quadrilateral layout and the skilful brickwork reflect continuity with local architectural traditions.

The integrative design approach is registered in every aspect of the project, and at every scale. The imbrication of outdoor and indoor spaces, together with the treatment of the roofscape, make this an unusual and innovative building. With its spaces sunk into the ground and the vegetation growing on its roofs, the compound blends beautifully into the natural surroundings. Its relationship to the landscape and to history and archaeology is remarkable in every way.

An attention to detail, to the human scale, is expressed in the simplicity of the well-designed furniture, in the creation of a series of small pavilions and reflecting pools, and in the landscaping elements. All help to create a friendly atmosphere, supporting the building's function of empowering a marginalised rural community living on a precarious floodplain.

While every aspect of this project is local – local inspiration, local builders, local materials, local architect, local NGO – its architectural value and qualities are undeniably universal and merit both appreciation and attention.

Client
Friendship NGO, Dhaka, Bangladesh:
Runa Khan, executive director
Rifiquzzaman Pollob, manager – field operations
Antim Kumar Paul, assistant manager – field operations

Architect
Kashef Chowdhury/URBANA, Dhaka, Bangladesh:
Kashef Mahboob Chowdhury, principal
Anup Kumar Basak, Sharif Jahir Hossain, design team
Matiur Rahman, structural engineer
SM Hafizur Rahman, engineer
Albab Yafez Fatmi, Sharijad Hasan, construction managers
Ahsanul Haque Ratan, Amrul Hasan, supervising engineers
Nahidur Rahman, site engineer
Zafar Ahmed, electrical design

Contractor
M/S Golam Mostofa Ltd, Dhaka, Bangladesh:
Golam Mostofa, proprietor

Plumbing Design
SEA-Consult, Bangkok, Thailand:
Phansak Thew, Jongsak Kuntonsurakan

Project Data
Built area: 3,053 m^2
Cost: 900,000 USD
Commission: May 2008
Design: May 2008–December 2010
Construction: December 2010–December 2011
Completion: December 2011

Kashef Chowdhury
The son of a civil engineer, Kashef Mahboob Chowdhury graduated in architecture from the Bangladesh University of Engineering and Technology (BUET) in 1995. He established the practice URBANA in partnership with Marina Tabassum in 1995 and, from 2004, has continued as the sole principal of the firm. He has a studio-based practice whose works find root in history with a strong emphasis on climate, materials and context – both natural and human. Projects in the studio are given extended time for research so as to reach a high level of innovation and original expression. Works range from the conversion of a ship and low-cost raised settlements in *chars* to a training centre, mosque, art gallery, museum, residences and multifamily housing, as well as corporate head offices. Kashef Chowdhury teaches both at home and abroad. In 2006, he attended a Glenn Murcutt masterclass in Sydney, Australia. He also takes an active interest in art and has worked as a professional photographer. Chowdury has designed and published three books: *Around Dhaka,* 2004; *Plot Number Fifty Six*, 2009 and *The Night of Fifteen November, 2011* – a photographic and recorded account of some survivors of Cyclone Sidr in the coastal areas of Bangladesh.

Website
www.kashefchowdhury-urbana.com

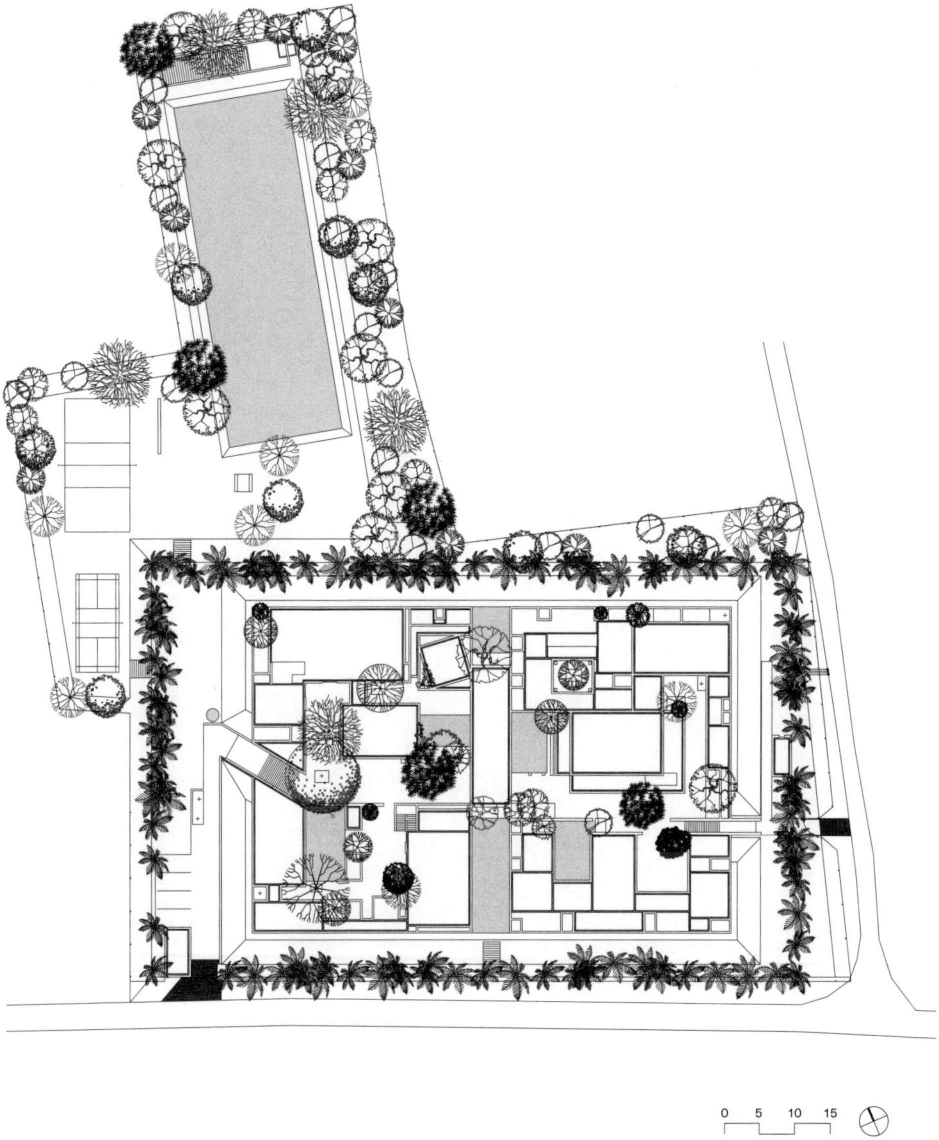
0 5 10 15

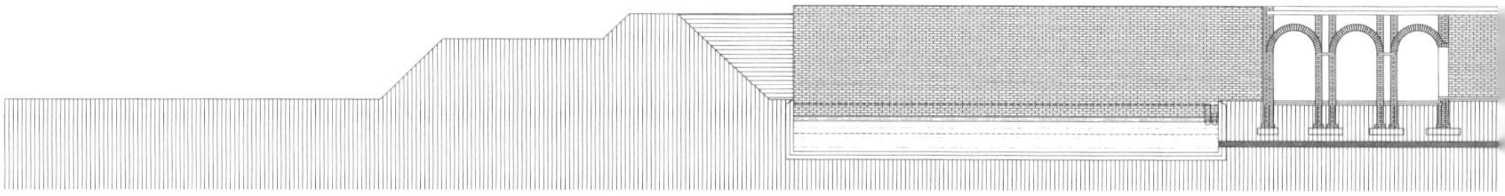

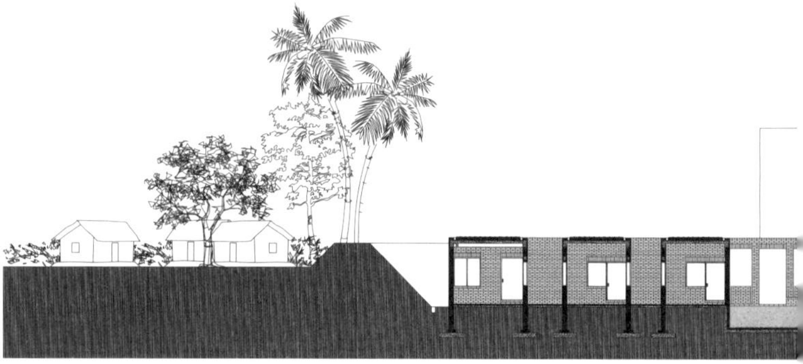

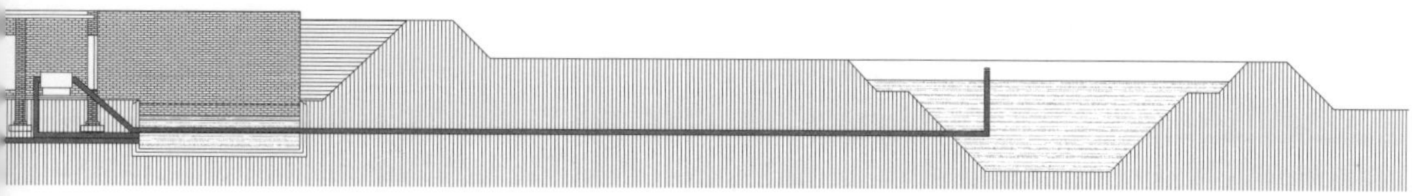

0
5
10
15

CONSERVATION

Conservation and adaptive reuse can play a significant role in the revitalisation of older buildings, serving to re-enact and reinforce their connection to the past and link them to the future. But the question of conservation is complex and the boundaries between conservation, preservation and reconstruction often seem fraught with contradictions. When faced with an important historic building what is the best strategy for conservation, what are the limits of rehabilitation? Projects such as the Manouchehri House in Iran or the Nasrid Tower in Spain approach the question of repair from different perspectives and yet both result in making important contributions, reanimating what would otherwise have been seen as mere ruins.

Micro Yuan'er Children's Library and Art Centre

Beijing, China

The hutongs of Beijing are fast disappearing. The residential compounds, with their layering of spaces and multiple courtyards, are often viewed as messy and insalubrious – almost as slums. If they find a place in the modern city, it is often in sanitised form, as a tourist attraction, filled with boutiques. The attempt to find a new use for this traditional building form – one that would benefit the local community – motivated this proposal for a space that would serve both the pupils from the nearby primary school and the hutong's remaining, mostly elderly, residents. Besides a children's library and exhibition space, the centre hosts a local handicrafts studio and classes in painting and dance.

Key to the design was the renovation and reuse of existing elements in the courtyard, which included informal add-on structures, such as kitchens. The massing follows the conditions found at the site, and the height of the boxes is dictated by the height of the roof around them. Gathering together all the masses and activities is a giant Scholar tree, perhaps 600 years old – as old as the courtyard itself.

The redesigned buildings in the centre of the courtyard have a lightweight steel structure and a 'floating' foundation – hollow steel beams simply laid on the ground – to protect the roots of the tree. The materials – chosen to blend with the urban surroundings – are principally grey bricks, both new and recycled, and, for the library, concrete mixed with Chinese ink – an innovation tested here for the first time.

Inside the library, windows frame unusual views out into the courtyard and follow the interior functions – as, for example, in the glazed reading nook that children reach by climbing some steps. The adaptable furniture – seating that can become an ad-hoc table or a 'secret cave', say – accommodates the spontaneity of childhood.

On the outside, the insertion of an outdoor staircase alongside each structure creates viewing platforms amid the tree's branches where the users of the courtyard – children and adults alike – can survey the neighbourhood and enjoy a breath of rare, chlorophyll-laced air.

Citation

Urbanisation in China has a complex relation with the past. How do you move forward while recognising the values of the built heritage? The response to this question has often led to a stark contrast between the old and the new, with the latter being seen as the sole marker of progress. Yet some have sought alternative strategies for urbanisation. Increasingly there is a call for a more nuanced consideration of the old and the existing, as potentially indispensable parts of urban developments.

The Micro Yuan'er Children's Library and Art Centre is an exemplary representative of the modification and adaptive reuse of a historic building. In Beijing, as in other places, a growing number of hutongs are being restored. But this hutong is not a typical restoration project. By providing new structures and new public uses in the middle of the building's courtyard, it entwines the private lives of the older inhabitants with the public use of a new children's library and art centre.

The architectural strategy of this modest but highly articulate intervention is to use the existing buildings and landscape as the armature for the new construction. The use of a limited palette of materials, such as brick, wood and glass, helps the space of the courtyard to become denser through the addition of the new structures.

The hutong provides an example of how the adaptive reuse of an older building can become the basis for a new form of micro-urbanism that constructs productive reciprocities between the private and the public. This is an approach that can be potentially replicated in other locations and within a diversity of communities.

全款购房
平房、四合院、公
房、私房均可，代
办过户，刘先生：
15652652686

Client
Beijing Dashilar – Liulichang Cultural Development Ltd, Beijing, China:
Jia Rong, director

#8 Cha'er Hutong Inhabitants
Wang ZengQi, Giao DaZhen, Man WeiGuo, Feng YuBao, Zhang JianKun, Beijing, China

Architect
ZAO/standardarchitecture, Beijing, China:
Zhang Ke, principal
Zhang Mingming, Fang Shujun, Ao Ikegami, Huang Tanyu, Margret Domko, Ilaria Positano, project team

Contractors
Liu Shanjie, Beijing, China
Wang Changjun, Beijing, China
Wang Zhanjun, Beijing, China

Project Data
Total area: 145 m^2
Cost: 105,000 USD
Commission: September 2012
Design: September 2012–July 2014
Construction: March 2014–December 2015
Completion: September 2014–December 2015

Zhang Ke
Zhang Ke received his master's degree in architecture from the Harvard Graduate School of Design, having previously studied at Tsinghua University in Beijing. He is the founder of studio ZAO/standardarchitecture, a new-generation design firm engaged in practices of planning, architecture, landscape and product design. Based on a wide range of completed buildings and landscapes over the past ten years, the studio has emerged as the most critical and realistic practice among the young generation of Chinese architects and designers.

Consciously distancing itself from many of the other 'typical' young-generation architects who are swallowed up by a trend of noise-making, the office remains detached in a time of media frenzy and their focus is consistently positioned to enable the realisation of urban visions and ideas. Although ZAO/standardarchitecture's built works often involve exceptionally provocative visual results, their buildings and landscapes are always rooted in their historic and cultural settings, the outcomes produced through a process of intellectual debate.

Website
www.standardarchitecture.cn
www.z-a-o.cn

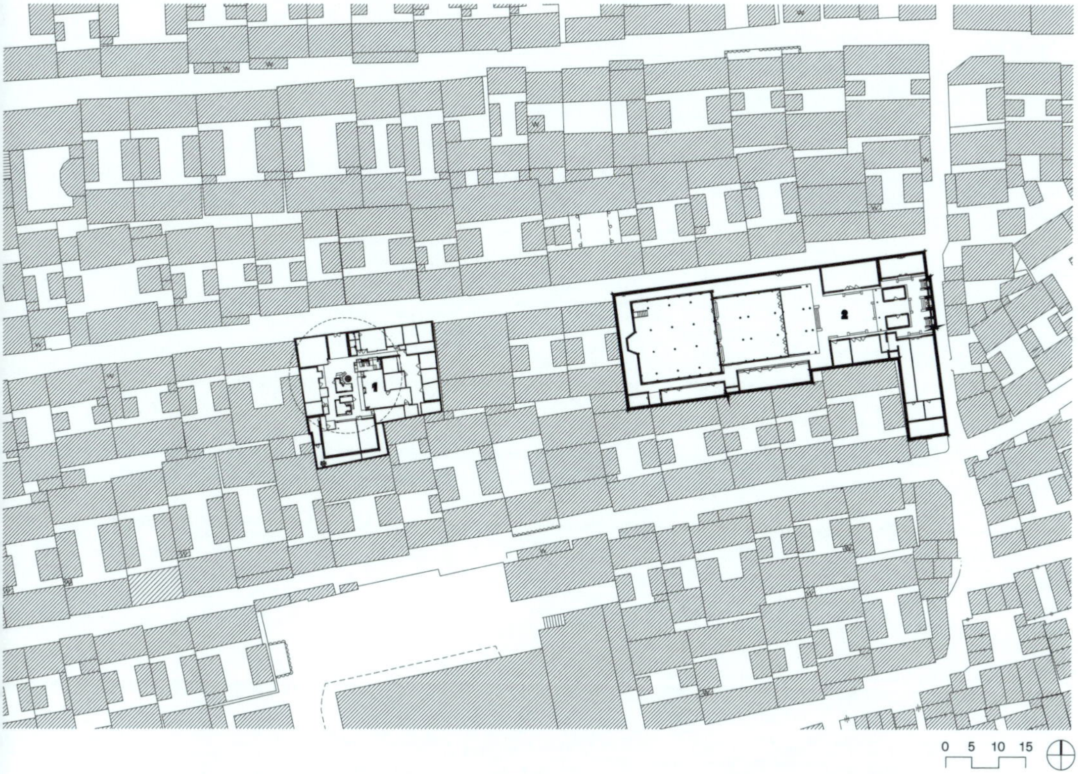
0 5 10 15

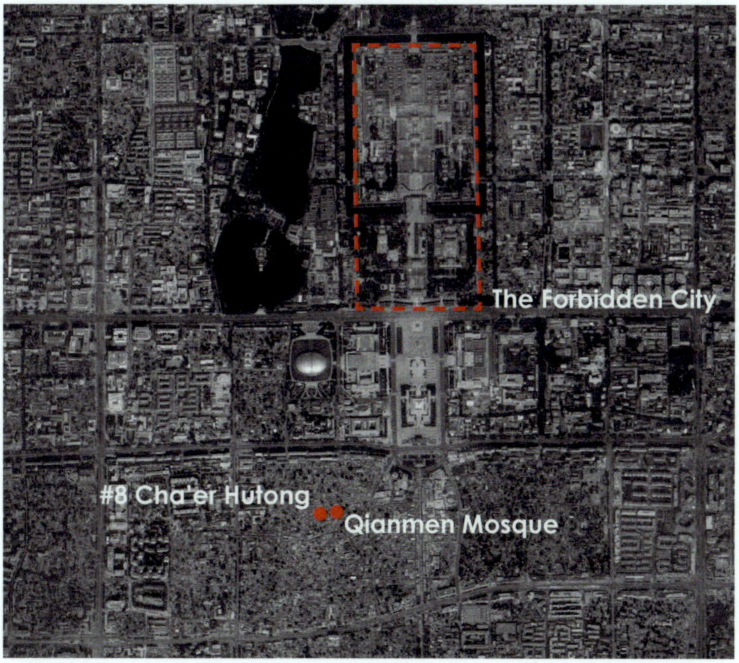
The Forbidden City
#8 Cha'er Hutong
Qianmen Mosque

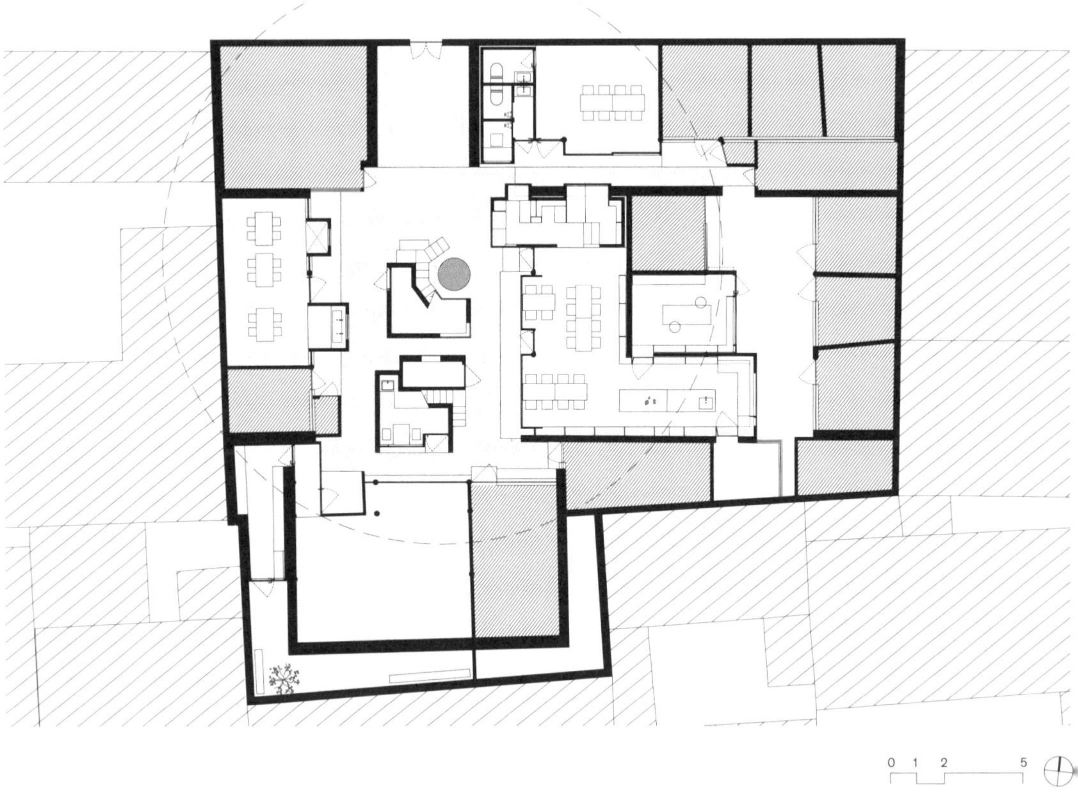
0 1 2 5

0
1
2
5

CONSTRUCTION

Construction is an indispensable part of architecture, and the basis for producing the significant and varied physical and perceptual conditions that help shape our relation to the work. A case in point is the construction of the Bait ur Rouf Mosque in Dhaka, where the variations in the handling of the brickwork produce spatial characteristics that – without reverting to symbolism – result in a building of immense atmosphere. Material construction constructs a sacred space, a situation appropriate for prayer. Brickwork is also used in the outer facade of the 40 Knots, an apartment building in Iran, to create a liminal spatial doubling of the building's outer skin and, through this, a form of veiling of the interior/exterior relations.

Bait ur Rouf Mosque

Dhaka, Bangladesh

An adherence to the essential – both in the definition of the space and the means of construction – was crucial in formulating the design of Bait ur Rouf Mosque. With land donated by her grandmother and modest funds raised by the local community, the architect has created an elemental place for meditation and prayer.

The irregularly shaped site is covered by a high plinth, which not only protects against flooding but provides a gathering place set apart from the crowded street below. On top of the plinth sits the mosque, a perfect square, 23 m × 23 m and 7.6 m high. Within this square is a cylinder, displaced to the northwest corner of the perimeter wall to create additional depth for the colonnade and the ablution area on the south- and east-facing sides respectively. And within this cylinder is in turn a smaller square, 16.75 m × 16.75 m and 10.6 m high – that is, 3 m taller than the perimeter wall. Rotated within the cylinder to orientate itself with the qibla, this pavilion contains the prayer hall, which is separated from the rest of the building by open-to-sky lightwells.

There are two structural systems in place – the load-bearing brick walls that define the outer perimeter and the smaller spaces, and the reinforced-concrete frame that spans the column-free prayer hall. The brick walls exploit the depth between the outer square and the inner cylinder, allowing for buttressing in the interstitial space. This in turn makes it possible for panels between the load-bearing structure to have a *jali* of brick, leaving out alternate bricks and rotating them. In the prayer hall itself a simple vertical gap in the brick denotes the direction of the qibla, but the recess is splayed so that worshippers are not distracted by sight lines onto the busy street. What they see instead is sunlight bouncing off the wall behind. Awash with light, open to the elements, the mosque 'breathes'.

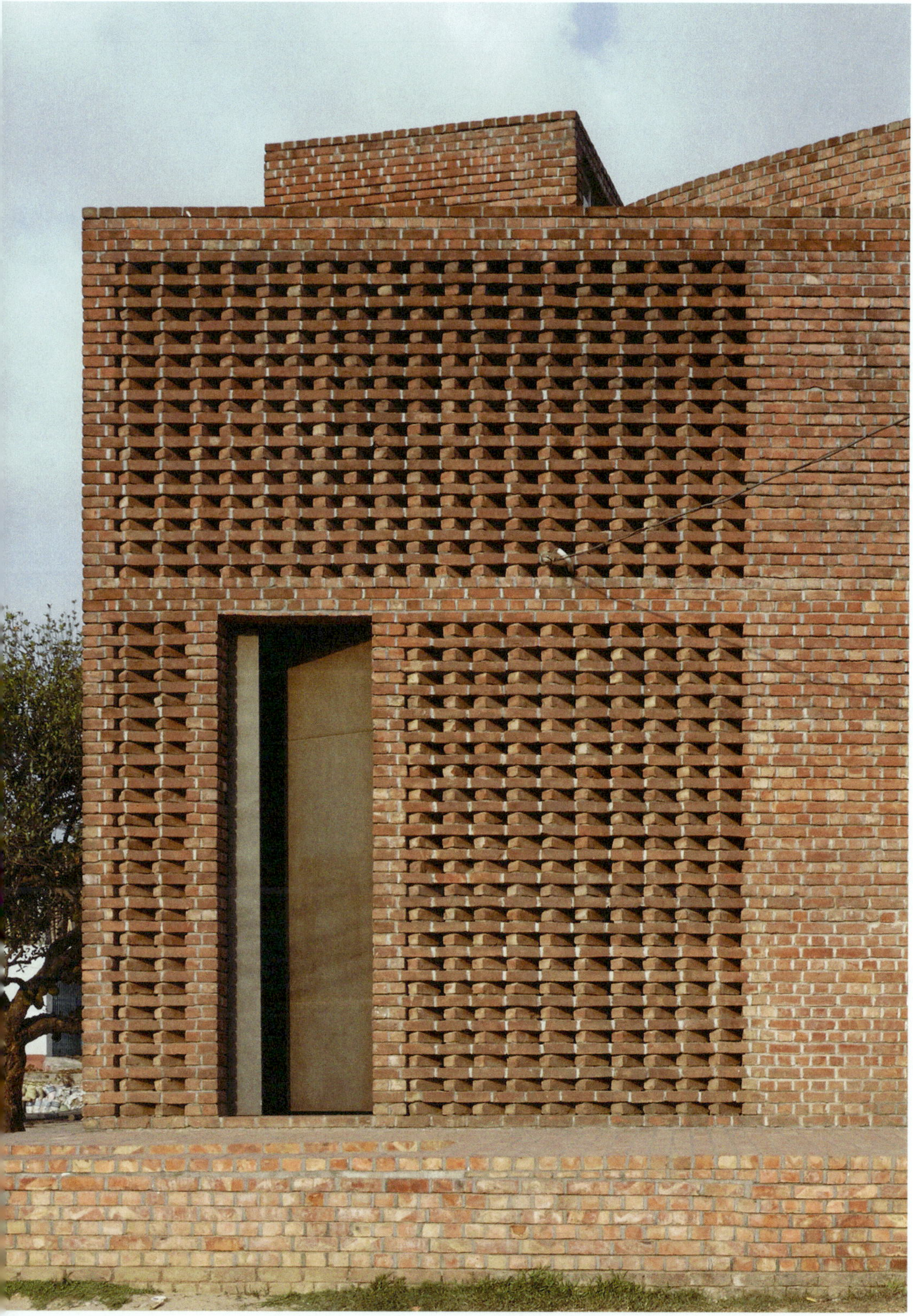

Bait ur Rouf Mosque, Dhaka, Bangladesh

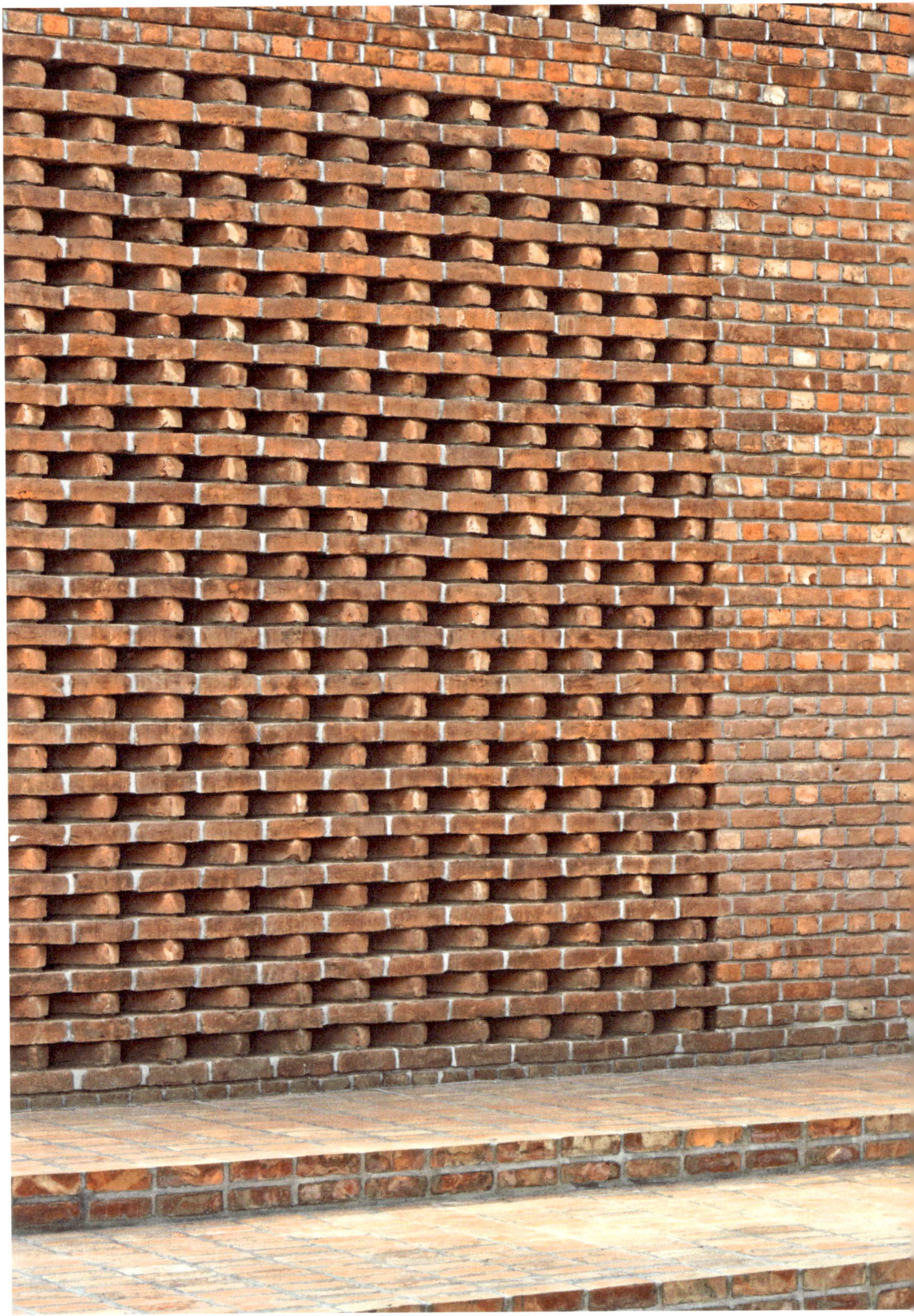

Citation

In a transitional area caught between urban hyper-density and rural proximity, the terracotta mosque is an exquisitely proportioned building that is both elegant and eternal. Funded primarily by community donors, the mosque design challenges the status quo and understands that a space for prayer should elevate the spirit. The mosque does so through the creation of an interior space that is rich with light and shadow but at the same time possesses a robust simplicity that allows for deep reflection and contemplation in prayer.

The mosque appears to be inspired by multiple sources – one essentially traditional reference is to the heritage of the formal terracotta brick structures of the Bengal Sultanate of the fifteenth century; another inspiration is the Capitol complex built by Louis Kahn in Dhaka.

The quality of construction frequently raises the quality of life. Nowhere is this more apparent than in the Bait ur Rouf Mosque, which contains an intricate geometric layering of space – a square prayer chamber contained within cylindrical walls, which are in turn enclosed by a square terracotta brick structure that serves as the austere public face of the building. Within the prayer chamber, the architect has created a delicate interplay of bare walls textured in red brick and pierced by shafts of light that create an abstract, almost primeval symbolism when viewed in conjunction with the spots of light that punctuate the surface of the bare floors at different moments of the day. This abstract symbolism is undiluted by conventional forms of mosque architecture. Gone are the dome and the ever-prevalent minarets, the decorative panels of designed relief and calligraphy. In their place stand intricately structured brick walls that imbue the structure with a unique aura of spirituality.

Bait ur Rouf Mosque, Dhaka, Bangladesh

Clients
Sufia Khatun, Dhaka, Bangladesh

Marina Tabassum, Dhaka, Bangladesh

Bait ur Rouf Mosque Committee, Dhaka, Bangladesh: Mohammad Abdul Hai, head and treasurer; Zulfiqer Ali Hyder, member; Jamal Abdul Naser, member

Architect
Marina Tabassum Architects, Dhaka, Bangladesh: Marina Tabassum, principal
Asaduzzaman Chowdhury, Tomal, Chowdhury, Hysum Mohammad Neville, Nazmus Saquib Chowdhury, Sabrina Aftab, Kaniz Saima Tuly, Shawly Samira, Sadia Afroze, Hassan Mohammad Rakib, Rahfatun Nisa Nova, project team

Structural Engineer
Daud Khalid Sarwar, Dhaka, Bangladesh

Electrical Engineer
Mohammad Rafiqul Islam, Dhaka, Bangladesh

Site Engineer
Bazlur Rahman, Dhaka, Bangladesh

Brick and Concrete Work
Shariful Islam, brick mason, Dhaka, Bangladesh

Terrazzo, Tile and Floor
Mohammad Esharul, Dhaka, Bangladesh

Project Data
Site area: 755 m^2
Ground floor area: 700m^2
Cost: 150,000 USD
Commission: April 2005
Design: June 2005–August 2006
Construction: September 2007–July 2012
Occupancy: September 2012

Marina Tabassum
Marina Tabassum graduated from Bangladesh University of Engineering and Technology (BUET) in 1995. The same year, with Kashef Mahboob Chowdhury, she founded URBANA, an architecture practice based in Dhaka. In 1997, her second year into practice, the firm won a prestigious national competition to design the Independence Monument of Bangladesh and the Liberation War Museum.

In 2005, Tabassum ended her ten-year partnership in URBANA to establish MTA (Marina Tabassum Architects). MTA began its journey in the quest to establish a language of architecture that is contemporary to the world yet rooted to the place. The practice is consciously kept and retained at an optimum size, and projects undertaken are carefully chosen and are limited by number per year.

Marina Tabassum is the academic director of the Bengal Institute for Architecture, Landscapes and Settlements. She has conducted design studios in BRAC University since 2005. She taught an Advanced Design Studio as visiting professor at the University of Texas.

Tabassum has lectured and presented her works and ideas on architecture at various prestigious international architectural events. She has curated exhibitions and directed architecture symposia in Dhaka, Bangladesh. Her project the Pavilion Apartment in Dhaka was shortlisted for an Aga Khan Award in 2004. Tabassum received an Ananya Shirshwa Dash award which recognised the top ten women of Bangladesh in 2004.

Website
www.mtarchitekts.com

0
50
100
150

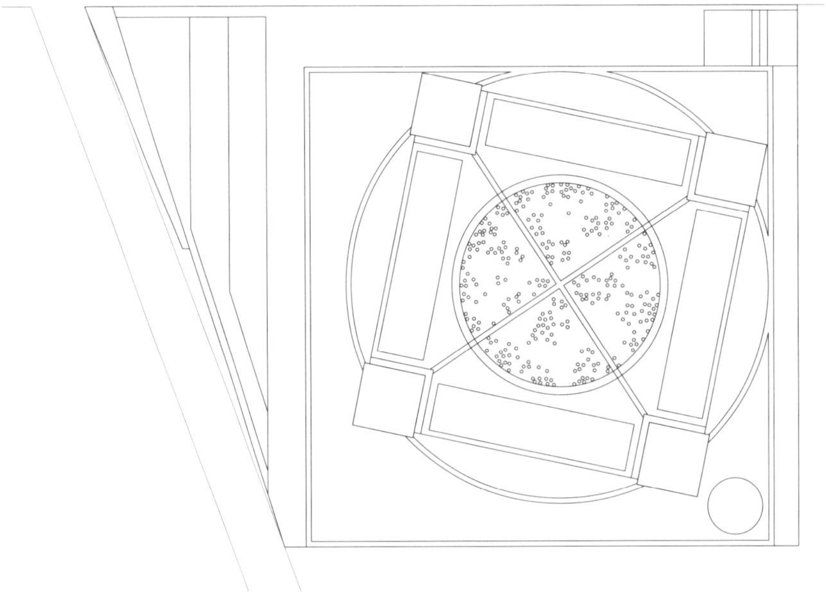

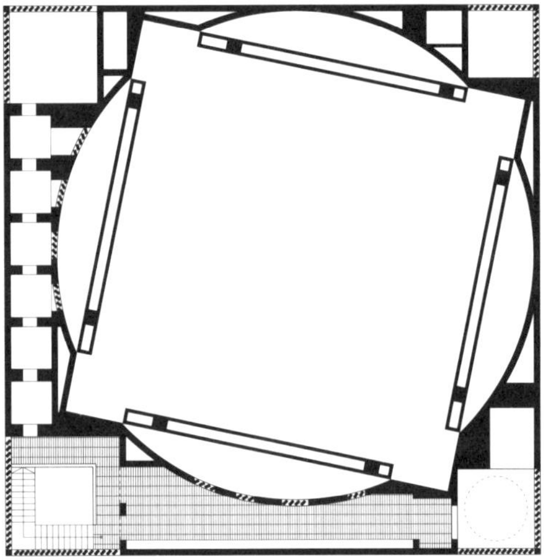

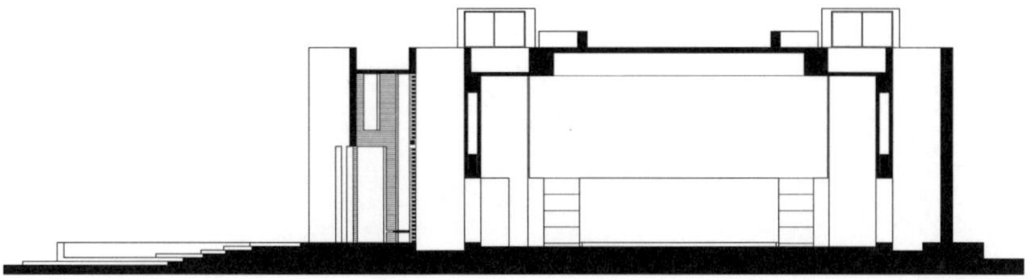

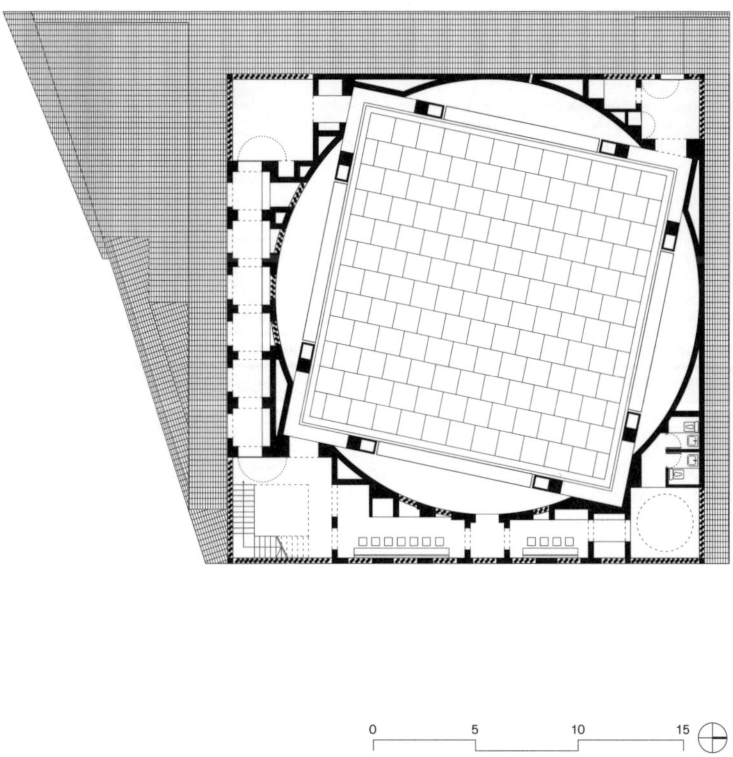
0
5
10
15

Parallel Readings in Contemporary Mosque Architecture and Bait ur Rouf

Emre Arolat

It was the first time that he'd been to my office, even though his family and mine had a business relationship that went back many years. I sat opposite him, trying to put aside all my prejudices. I was really curious as to what he might say, but in truth I didn't hold out much hope that we'd be able to come to any sort of agreement.

During the early minutes of the encounter we were like two boxers sizing each other up. From his briefcase he removed a file with a blue plastic cover and set it down, lining it up neatly with the edges of the desk. Taking his mobile from the inside pocket of his jacket, he switched it to silent and then smiled at me with a look that said, 'Well, go ahead and open it.'

On the first page there was a rather ineptly framed photograph of what appeared to be – by the looks of its minaret and dome – a replica of a classical Ottoman mosque. The lower part of the main structure was faced in what I supposed was a local claystone; the upper part was rendered and painted in a colour that attempted to match the stone. My visitor started the con-versation by saying that they had completed the work the previous year. And if you looked very closely, you could just make out that a section of the qibla wall was clad in greenish curtain glass. That part had apparently drawn much criticism; neither local worshippers nor the more conservative wing of the family had completely come to terms with it, he said. I could see why. It didn't have much to say for itself. I tried to change the subject, but my visitor persisted. That bit of glass was an important advance in mosque architecture, he asserted – and evidence that one part of the family, at least, was open to innovation. Fortunately he didn't press the point much further...

It would not be amiss to say that the intellectual framework of contemporary architecture is informed by a bias towards innovation. Though the success of this strategy in many parts of the world may be moot, both architectural practice and education turn their face towards the future. Of course, this is not a bias that originates solely within the profession. In the context of global capitalism, in which a climate of competition reigns supreme, architects are often egged on by investors in search of novelty. In broad brushstroke terms, then, we could talk about a great divide within the profession. On the one hand, you have a small group who could truly be described as adhering to an innovative design process, or pursuing an inter-rogatory and critical stance. On the other, you have the vast majority of the profession, for whom the practice of architecture has been reduced to a kind of formalistic acrobatics. Acting as the technical agents of capital, the members of this group supply grist to the mills of the market. And when it comes to the creation of iconic works intended to nourish interest in 'appearance' and, transcending that, 'spectacle' (one of the vogues of our neoliberal era), then those are waters in which we sometimes willingly swim – and sometimes desperately thrash about.

However clichéd or passé this may seem to many, I still value an approach that is not just oriented towards visions of the future – or simply towards the needs of the present – but is also nourished by the cultural influences of previous eras. For me, the architectural design process, and the intellectual framework that supports it, can only be enriched through their association with the broadest possible range of multitemporal and multilayered criteria. Moreover, the relationship of a work of architecture to past tradition or, conversely, to futuristic fantasies, need not be viewed in simple terms of opposition, but rather should be exploited as a source of richness – as a source of dialectical thinking, which has been an indispensable paradigm of architectural practice through the ages.

This is the background against which we might now consider various aspects of the matter of mosque architecture and how they relate to the tension between mainstream expectations and contemporary architectural practice.

I turned over the page to find a map that showed the place where the mosque was to be built. The site was trapezoidal. A road passed just behind it, while the front and sides were clear of any other structure. Putting on my glasses, I examined the contours of the land. A gentle slope led down to the site from the road. On the last page of the file, a photograph caught my eye: a lush green valley, knee-deep grass, a lake resembling a silver tray gleaming in the sunlight and extending as far as the eye could see. 'Not here!', I said to myself, fearing what was to come next: I was all but certain that he would ask for a replica of a classical Ottoman mosque – a project that I would not want to take on. Then a sense of regret washed over me. I wished I'd never seen that enchanting landscape. Once again smiling with a look which suggested that he understood how much I'd been affected, my visitor observed my astonishment without uttering a word. I recalled how just few weeks earlier I had explained to my students that it was important for an architect to love the site of a project he was working on. Some of them, I'm sure, sniggered quietly behind my back at that. At least they couldn't see me now. I would never have imagined that loving a place would also carry with it the risk of making it so very hard to lose.

After a long pause we resumed our conversation. He was aware of the views that I had previously expressed on the subject: about how hard it was to design a new mosque in Turkey, how such an undertaking was a battle that was in any case impossible to win, how much I despaired of the simplistic conservatism that typically defined conventional expectations of mosque architecture. He said he had been especially moved by my assertion that there was in fact no formal description anywhere of what an Islamic house of worship ought to be: neither in the Qur'an itself, nor in any other text that deserved to be taken seriously. After this brief – and to me utterly astonishing – exposition, he declared that he had come to me to have 'some other kind' of mosque built. That was all he knew and all he was going to say. The rest was up to me. I sat there stunned.

It really is true that Islam makes absolutely no prescriptions concerning the formal features of houses of worship. The Qur'an says nothing about the shapes of minarets or the dimensions of mihrabs; neither is there any mention of a dome. The sole stipulation is as pragmatic as it is straightforward: one must worship in a place that is clean. That being so, one could regard the whole world as a potential house of worship. No decorative element nor any symbolic or physical object is needed either to perform the *salaat* (prescribed liturgy) or to pray. Such a holistic approach – or intellectual minimalism, if you will – is also intrinsic to the core principles of Islamic mysticism. For even though rather little attention has been given to it in recent years, humility is one of the basic tenets of Islamic philosophy. Moreover a mosque is not supposed to be a venue for grand rituals and ceremonies, of the kind found in many other religions. Rather, it is a kind of public space in which people come together and worship, or a place to which a person comes to commune with and contemplate sometimes his Creator and sometimes just his own inner world. How one is supposed to worship in Islam is much more straightforward than is the case in other monotheistic religions. Indeed, not even an imam (prayer-leader) is needed in most situations.

When the substance of Islamic philosophy is considered carefully in light of these facts, mosque architecture might seem to be one area in which architects ought to enjoy the greatest freedom and even produce some of their most original work. But back here in the 'real' world, the one in which we live, the truth is quite different – and has been for many centuries. For example, if you want to build a new and modern mosque here in Turkey, the first obstacle you encounter is the continuing attachment to the physical form of the classical Ottoman mosque of the sixteenth century. Over the course of hundreds of years the structural elements of this typology have been repeated endless times, each repetition grinding down a little more the very notion that 'some other kind' of mosque might even be possible. Any would-be designer who proposes a solution that does not include circular-shafted, conical-capped minarets, or who dares to have a sanctuary unadorned by a central dome, finds themselves hobbled – bound hand and foot, as it were. Even questioning the conformism that underlies the social consensus that has grown up is like swimming upstream against a violent current; an effort to be undertaken only by the most intrepid. The very issue of mosque design dropped off – or was expunged from – the agenda of serious architecture as the brilliance of the Ottoman empire waned. The overwhelming majority of mosques built thereafter were either mediocre affairs or else no more than imitations of far superior works.

In his article 'Profession of Faith', Uğur Tanyeli describes how 'recent Turkish religious architecture and the historiographical-ideological assumptions of believers are intimately bound together. Regarding themselves as direct descendants of the exalted Ottomans, today's mosque builders express their devotion through ambitious construction programmes that favour quantity over quality.'[1] And the principal function of the mosque, for those builders assuming the mantle of Süleymaniye the Magnificent, is 'to visualise the prevailing ideology of nationalism and religion within space, inculcating an inherently nostalgic and retrospective approach'. Tanyeli then adds: 'Despite Islam's liturgical simplicity, new mosques in Turkey are charged with a complex ideological and political burden. The modern mosque is an icon or a complex of icons, the main aim of which is to support *realpolitik*.'

Ample evidence in support of Tanyeli's arguments is provided by Çamlıca Mosque, now nearing completion in İstanbul. Set on a lofty hill with a commanding view of the Bosphorus, it is in turn visible from practically everywhere in the city – a gigantic structure with a central dome, 72 m high and 35 m wide, supplemented by 70 more domes of various sizes and no less than six minarets. The design and the construction works have been personally overseen by the President of the Republic of Turkey himself. Not much is known about the architect of the mosque, which has been built to deliberately mimic Süleymaniye, one of the most important works of the sixteenth-century Ottoman architect Sinan. It is planned to mark the opening of Çamlıca Mosque with a grand ceremony, with the leading heads of state of the Islamic world in attendance.

From the outset I had little hope that this mosque would ever be approved, much less built – as I repeatedly made clear to the people working with me on the project, as a way of tempering their inevitable disappointment. Our task, I told them, was to do what we knew was right, and to create the best possible expression of the underlying idea that we had come up with after many months of mulling over Islamic philosophy. We should not concern ourselves with any more than that, I said. The worst that could happen would be that the first mosque that we'd ever been asked to design would also be the last.

They arrived early one morning, about 20 of them. They'd even brought along the local county mufti. Because of the light reflected off the projector screen I was able to see their faces and how they reacted to what I said during my presentation. While a few of them started grumbling at my references to 'contemplation', 'the essence of worship' and 'topographical conformity', some seemed to be pleased by what they were seeing and hearing. It occurred to me that this project was going to split the family in two. A thick silence descended when the presentation came to an end. One of my colleagues switched on the lights. Eyes darted left and right, but nobody said a word. 'I wish they'd just up and leave and get this agony over with', I thought to myself. Then the mufti finally spoke up, declaring that he wanted to pray in such a mosque as soon as possible. Just a year after this presentation, a miniscule mosque was built in a grassy glen leading down to a silvery lake on the outskirts of İstanbul. From the outside you hardly notice it's there.

Several years have gone by since the completion of Dhaka's Bait ur Rouf Mosque, designed by Marina Tabassum. Shortlisted in 2016 by the AKAA Master Jury, of which I am a member, the building subsequently became an Award-winner with hardly any reservations at all. The contrast between the structure's solidity and the chaotic physical context in which it is situated; the masterful use of simple, locally available materials; the primordial character of its interior and the way in which that interior is naturally ventilated and suffused with daylight; the monumentality that the mosque projects, notwithstanding its simplicity and its modest scale – all are worthy of every sort of praise. It is also very important that the mosque has been taken to heart by its community. The building's architect has said that the backbone of her design was informed by the core principles of Islamic worship, and that the structure was derived from the kinds of formally unpretentious dwellings that ordinary people have been putting up for thousands of years. Decrying the serious degeneration of vernacular mosque architecture in Bangladesh in recent years, Tabassum adds that she designed Bait ur Rouf Mosque with the idea of stitching the faded glory of the country's imperial mosque-building tradition together with the needs, materials and techniques of the present day.

The backstory to the design process is also rather interesting. Tabassum herself undertook the project as architect and builder, her grandmother having bequeathed a plot of land on which to build a mosque. Although she diligently coordinated all aspects of the undertaking, even acting as a fundraiser, she avoided putting herself in the limelight in any way. Her restraint made it all the more easy for the local community to identify with the mosque.

Marina Tabassum is now seeking further funds with which to finance the construction of accommodation for the mosque's imam and a small schoolhouse immediately adjacent to the main building. She might even add a minaret, since the congregation appears to want one. Thus does the Bait ur Rouf Mosque remind us that architecture is – and always has been – a living process and an undertaking which can make a positive contribution to social progress.

It also reminds me of the last sentence of the brilliant article that Oleg Grabar wrote on present-day Muslim communities' perceptions of mosque architecture: 'Perhaps the future of the Muslim faith lies in local communities rather than in nation-states.'[2]

Staring in horror at the Çamlıca Mosque, I can't help but think, and hope, that he might be right.

1 Uğur Tanyeli, 'Profession of Faith', *Architectural Review,* August 2014, 33.
2 Oleg Grabar, 'The Mosque in Islamic Society Today', in Martin Frishman and Hassan Uddin Khan (eds), *The Mosque, History, Architectural Development & Regional Diversity* (London: Thames & Hudson, 1994), 245.

Architecture of the Essential

Nondita Correa Mehrotra

In this Award Cycle, two of the winning projects are in Bangladesh – the Bait ur Rouf Mosque, Dhaka and the Friendship Centre, Gaibandha. While different in many ways, both projects reflect the humble means of the communities that they serve. In both, the budget has been the disciplining criterion, forcing the architects to define what is fundamental to their buildings and to make the design simple in every way. It is this limitation that has created an 'Architecture of the Essential'.

Bait ur Rouf Mosque

The mosque is extremely elegant and has been exceptionally well executed on a modest budget. In approaching the design, the architect Marina Tabassum searched for the essence of a place of congregational prayer. For her, this is a space 'devoid of ritualistic and symbolic attributes', which is contemplative and 'evenly lit to enhance the feeling of all as equals', as a brotherhood praying towards the qibla. The mosque is inward-looking, as befits a place of meditation. In the large volume of the prayer hall, natural light pours down on the unplastered handmade brick walls, giving the interior a primordial character. Warm and rich in colour and texture, the light washes the space, which is the essence of sanctity.

This terracotta brick building is exquisitely scaled. Though small, it has an imposing presence and holds its corner in a fragmented, chaotic urban landscape. There are no views out from the prayer hall; all light enters from above. The construction and craftsmanship of the brick walls is exceptional. Taking every element of a mosque and giving it a modern voice, the building is a wonderfully contemporary expression of a timeless programme.

The Bait ur Rouf Mosque is exemplary as a small-scale participatory project for a community building, funded through charitable contributions. Yet what is even more admirable is the architectural expression. Here is the quintessential mosque, elegant yet elemental, with spaces that are direct, simple and robust, allowing the congregation to gather in prayer as equals.

Friendship Centre

The Friendship Centre, near the Brahma-Jamuna river, is a training facility for an NGO engaged in transformative work in northern Bangladesh, helping the rural communities who live on the floodplains and on sandbars that are destroyed every time this mighty river is in spate.

The conventional means of flood-proofing – which is to raise the building on 2.4 m of earth-fill and foundations – would have used up three-quarters of the budget. So the architect, Kashef Mahboob Chowdhury, chose instead to set the building directly on the low-lying land and to protect the entire site with an embankment that could be built and maintained for much less.

The basic and the fundamental lie at the core of this design process, as they do at the centre of the lives of the people the building serves. Within extreme limitations of means, there is a search for what Chowdhury describes as the 'luxury of light and shadows, of the economy and generosity of small spaces, and the joy of movement and discovery'.

The largest part of Bangladesh lies in the delta of the Ganges-Brahmaputra river system. In this landscape, the relationship of land to water is continuously negotiated, both by nature and in man-made interventions. The people of this region exist with the knowledge that, with every monsoon, the ravages of the river could destroy their lives, yet they stay here because the alluvial soil is rich with fresh silt deposits; they have no alternative means of subsistence. They live on *chars* (sandbars or riverine islands), too poor to have access to a boat, and isolated from the world except when the river is shallow enough to wade across.

The NGO Friendship has worked with these communities since it was founded in 2002 by Runa Khan. Initially the focus was on providing healthcare, with the help of a floating hospital. Over time, recognising that the broader goal of enabling these communities to gain control over their lives requires more than healthcare support alone, Friendship has progressively built its distinctive integrated development model, which includes health, nutrition; education; disaster management and infrastructure development; good governance; and sustainable economic development.[1]

I visited two of their sites, one on a char, where all the facilities could be dismantled – the structures are traditionally made of bamboo and thatch, but now also incorporate corrugated GI sheets. Friendship has started a school, supplied the people with boats, and found funding to help them raise cattle and goats and grow corn in the fields. It has provided looms and taught women weaving skills. While I was there, a group of women sat in a circle outside the health centre (a small examination room), participating in a session on personal hygiene. The young woman leading the group was trained at the Friendship Centre. I later learned that this char will have to be evacuated before this year's monsoon as it has shown signs of cracking and is certain to be destroyed by the river.

The second site was the floating hospital, a converted riverboat with operating theatres, an emergency room, etc. There were postoperative facilities on the riverbank, again built with materials that are easily dismantled. The hospital was staffed by local people, except for two doctors – a surgeon and an anaesthetist – and two nurses, who had come from France for two weeks. Every two weeks different doctors come in, and the boat moves downstream to provide healthcare to another group of villages.

Friendship realised that they needed a centre to train their staff, to include not only teaching spaces but also accommodation for trainees for the duration of the workshops. Architect Kashef Chowdhury says, 'We wanted to take this idea further and truly create a centre around which the activities of this wonderful organisation would revolve, but that could also serve as a place which brings people together. In this way the architecture needed to be simple and bare: a response to the economy of the region, and with a quality of calmness and serenity that echoes the nature of its riverine landscape setting.'[2]

The site of the Friendship Centre was a paddy field set slightly lower than the road, and part of a landscape that extends in all directions – lush green, studded with small sheds and low-cost structures. The centre blends beautifully with the architecture in the vicinity – very simple, temporary shelters made of bamboo, thatch and GI sheets, as well as homes in brick masonry, plastered and limewashed, built on raised mounds of earth on the edges of the paddy fields. There are a few shops, some temporary, some permanent, at times lining both sides of the road. Chowdhury has also said that some of his inspiration came from the Buddhist monasteries in the area. The exposed brickwork, stark character and quadrilateral layout of the building all seem to speak of this influence.

After visiting these two buildings it was interesting to reflect on how strict economic constraints had been converted, in both projects, into strong aesthetic statements. Both works, the Bait ur Rouf Mosque and the Friendship Centre, are built in unplastered handmade brick – a rational decision, based on an economy of means, but also an aesthetic one. Terracotta is the most prominent building material in Bangladesh, in fact in all of Bengal. As there is very little stone available in the region, all construction of low-rise structures is in brick, usually loadbearing, or reinforced concrete frame with brick infill. There are thousands of brick kilns dotted across the country, as this is a large part of the informal economy. And while the majority of the brick structures are then rendered, buildings designed y modern architects are often in exposed concrete or exposed brick, erhaps because of the legacy of the architects who built here in the 1960s – uch as Louis Kahn (who designed the Capitol complex, Sher-e-Bangla Jagar), or Bangladesh's own Muzharul Islam, who created the basis for profession and an intellectual discipline.[3] In both of these projects he modernist aesthetic, combined with the use of local handmade bricks, as created a strong tectonic language – a redefining of an 'Architecture f the Essential' for the region.

From Friendship's mission statement, handout.

Interview in *UnCube*, 'The Luxury of Light and Shadows', February 2013.

Kazi K Ashraf, 'Muzharul Islam, Kahn and Architecture n Bangladesh', in H-U Khan (ed), *Minmar 31: Architecture in Development* (Singapore: Concept Media, 1989).

INFRASTRUCTURE

Far from being limited to large-scale technical structures such as highways and airports, infrastructure as a term has come to encompass a variety of structures of different scales performing different functions. The modest experimental Makoko Floating School in Nigeria investigates the potential of a floating structure to accommodate both the functions of a school and the daily lives of a group of children – an experiment not without risk. On the other hand the Tabiat Bridge in Iran is a massive piece of infrastructure intended more as a public space of leisure than as a bridge in the traditional sense. Infrastructure is increasingly becoming a critical public amenity. This is clearly the role of the Casa-Port New Railway Station in Morocco, a building of clarity that serves as a symbol of civic pride and of mobility.

Tabiat Pedestrian Bridge

Tehran, Iran

Tabiat Pedestrian Bridge spans a busy highway to connect two parks in a city with a very dense urban fabric and mostly utilitarian architecture. More than a point of connection between two discrete green zones, the bridge is a popular gathering place for the people of Tehran, offering numerous seating areas over its three levels and restaurants at either end. Like many such green spaces within urban areas, it has come to serve as a locus of identity for the city and its inhabitants.

The tree-shaped columns that support Tabiat Pedestrian Bridge echo the forms within the adjacent parks. Their locations were also carefully chosen to minimise the need to fell trees. And where the bridge meets Abo Atash Park, the structure is left open in three places to allow the trees to grow through it, creating the sense of one continuous green space.

Given the complex curving form of the three-dimensional truss, each of the steel elements had to be cut in a different shape, and this was carried out partly by CNC machine and partly by printing the unrolled shape from the 3D model. The tubes were cut, sandblasted and painted with primer in the workshop, then delivered to the site. During the whole process of construction, the flow of traffic on the highway continued uninterrupted.

Rather than focusing on the experience of those viewing the bridge from afar, the design is characterised by an inward-looking approach: the sequences of spaces are all centred around the users. The various deck levels are connected by continuous ramps at the bridge's southern end: the decks themselves are covered in Resysta, an imported fibre-reinforced hybrid material made from rice husks, common salt and mineral oil. The same material – which is both recyclable and weather-resistant – was used for the seating.

Citation

Tabiat Pedestrian Bridge is a breath of fresh air in an otherwise austere and haphazardly built area of Tehran. The challenge of connecting two parks separated by a highway is met with an approach that is exemplary in the context of an infrastructure project, not just in Tehran but perhaps anywhere in the world.

The apparent reinterpretation of the original brief, which called for a straightforward connection between two parks, has transformed a 'bridge' into a 'destination'. Inviting people to congregate, interact and appreciate the vista in every direction, the bridge has become a promenade and one of the most successful public spaces in modern Tehran.

The bridge's use of technology and integration of architecture and structure is commendable, particularly in the light of the challenges the team would have faced in the design and procurement stages of the project. Though the jury felt that there was scope for further aesthetic refinement of the structure, it acknowledged that some design decisions may have been influenced by the fact that the bridge lies in an area of high seismic activity.

In spite of this, the bridge displays a structural logic that is at once simple yet robust, orderly yet chaotic, but always functional, provocative and inviting. The physical footprint of the structure is minimised, with respect shown towards the existing trees and topography. The sophisticated layering of the bridge deck, which allows and encourages different activities, is commended by the jury.

Tabiat Pedestrian Bridge is a successful example of a calculated risk taken by a client, met with the youth and enthusiasm of a group of competent professionals whose work is commendable and deserving of recognition.

Client
Nosazi Abbasabad Co, Tehran Municipality, Tehran, Iran:
Seyed Javad Mirhosseini, head of architectural department (2008–2015)
Behnam Atabaki, managing director (2008–2011)
Ghasem Amouzandeh, deputy to managing director (2008–2011)

Architect
Diba Tensile Architecture, Tehran, Iran:
Leila Araghian, Alireza Behzadi, co-founders
Sahar Yasaei, associate
Mina Nikoukalam, Homa Soleimani, Farhad Elahi, Nader Naghipour, Kourosh Shirani, Adel Mohammadi, Masoud Momeni, Payam Golfeshan, project team

Structural Engineering
Maffeis Engineering SpA, Solagna, Italy:
Massimo Maffeis, Marco Grigoletto, Loris Frizon, structural engineers

Contractor
Shahid Rajaei Company, Tehran, Iran:
Mojtaba Keshtkar, Hossein Saemi, executive managers

Steel Structure Construction Sub-contractors
Azar Teif Sepahan Company, Tehran, Iran

Mashin Sazi Arak Company, Tehran, Iran

Consultants
Aram Shahriari, mechanical engineer, Tehran, Iran

Mahmoud Abdolhasani, electrical engineer, Tehran, Iran

Pouya Tarh Pars, local structural approver, Tehran, Iran

Construction Company
Azar Teif Sepahan Company, Tehran, Iran

Project Data
Total length of the bridge: 269 m
Total combined floor area: 7,950 m^2
Cost: 18,200,000 USD
Commission: September 2009
Design: September 2009–December 2010
Construction: October 2010–October 2014
Completion: October 2014

Diba Tensile Architecture
Diba Tensile Architecture, founded in 2005, was the first company in Iran to specialise in the design, fabrication and installation of membrane and tensile structures The main idea behind starting the firm was to bring a new specialty to the country's construction industry. The approach at Diba is to integrate architecture and structure with the maximum attention to detail and to the execution of a project, as well as to the quality of the spaces that are created. In 2008 Diba won the competition to design Tabiat Bridge, and since then it has undertaken larger scale projects with sophisticated structural characteristics in close cooperation with Maffeis Engineering SpA.

So far Diba has completed over 300 projects on various scales in Iran, structures that are specifically designed and constructed to meet client needs. These include bridges and open-air amphitheatres, monumental structures, building entrances and parking lots, as well as temporary structures such as sunshades, covers and gazebos. It continues to grow in both the design and construction of innovative projects.

Website
www.dibats.com

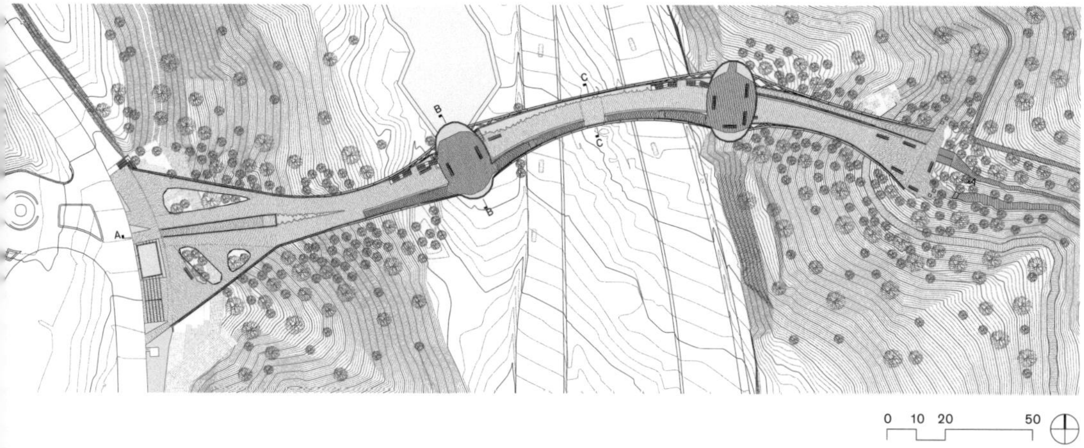
0 10 20 50

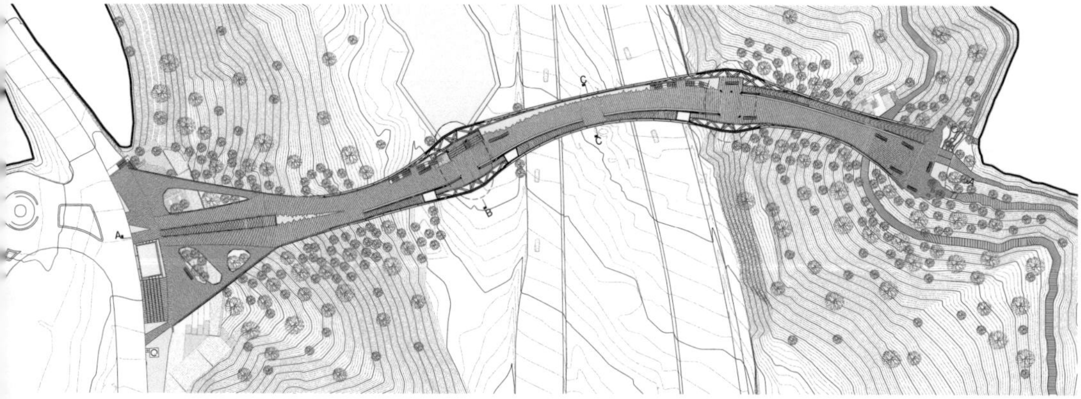

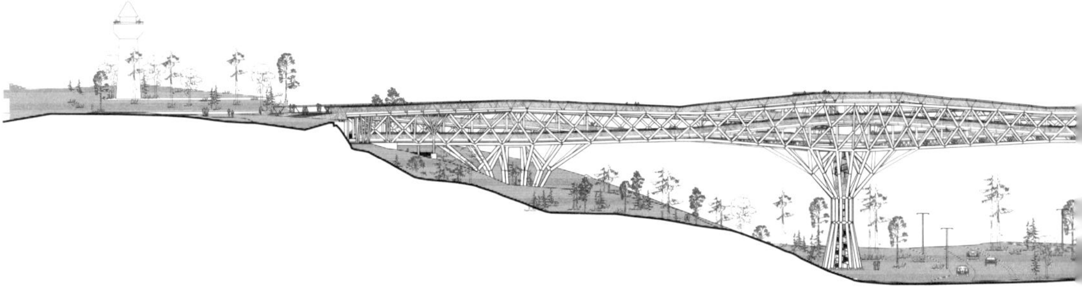

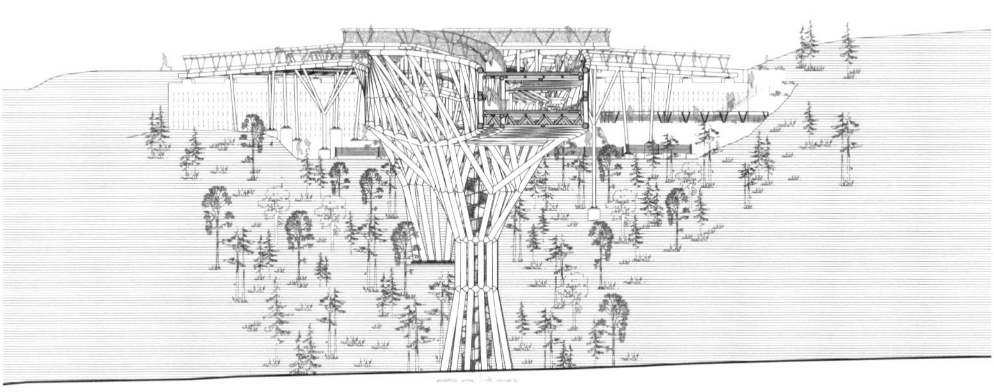

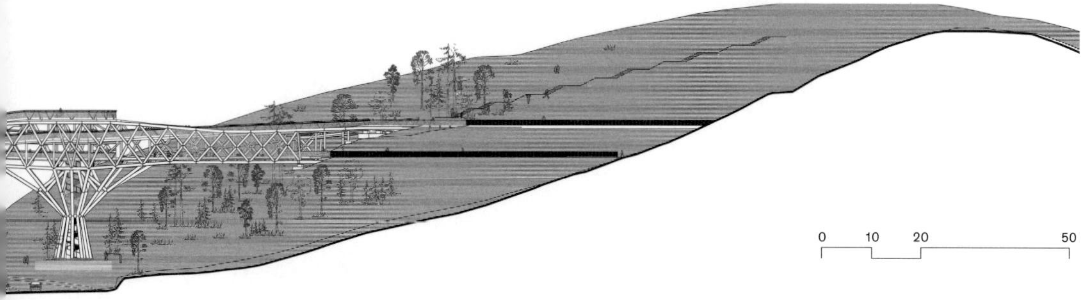
0
10
20
50

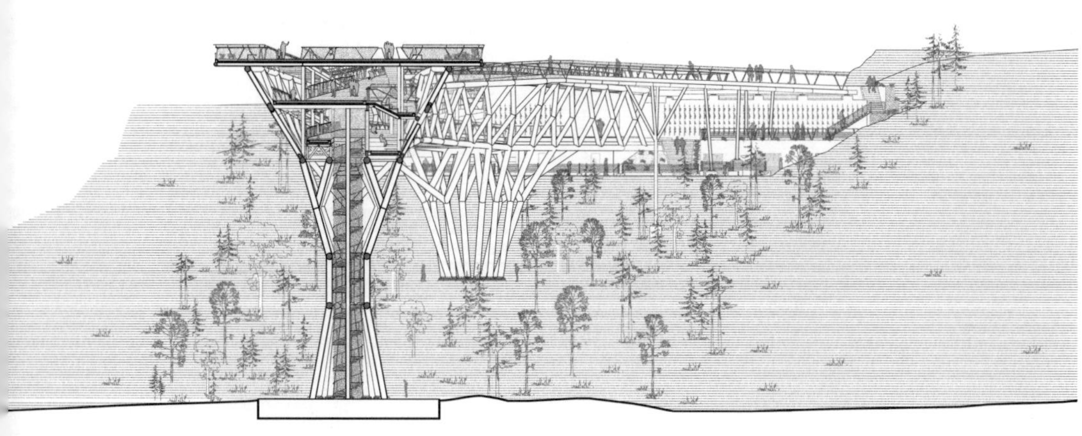
0
5
10
15

The Bridge

Hassan Radoine

Within the space of a few short years Tabiat Bridge has become one of the landmarks of Tehran. Set in the Abbasabad Hills, the 270-m-long pedestrian bridge spans over a valley to connect two public parks on either side of Modarres Avenue, one of the city's major highways. The location provides respite from the nightmare of traffic-jam Tehran, with views of the whole city and the spectacular backdrop of the Alborz Mountains. Designed as a place 'to stay' rather than simply 'to pass',[1] the bridge generates different experiences for its users day and night, in accordance with the principle (a revolutionary one, for Iran) that the pedestrian should have priority over the car.

It is striking to note that the bridge is located in the very same area of north Tehran that Mohammad Reza Shah earmarked for his new ceremonial urban centre – a large plaza and two boulevards lined with government and commercial buildings, master-planned by Llewelyn Davies International. Construction of the complex began in 1975, but was abruptly halted by the fall of the Pahlavi monarchy in 1979. An earlier proposal for the site, solicited from Louis Kahn and Kenzo Tange, was left unfinished when Kahn died in March 1974, while the master plan for Tehran (1966–70), prepared jointly by Victor Gruen and Farmanfarmaian Associates, also came to naught. All three proposals were responses to demands for the rapid modernisation of Tehran – demands that would lead the city into a 'tragedy of development'.[2]

In the late 1980s and early 1990s, as the country began to rebuild after the Islamic Revolution and the eight-year Iran–Iraq war, proposals by local firms paved the way for a final master plan, which was drawn up by Naqsh-e-Jahan Pars, the practice directed by Seyed Hadi Mirmiran. With its hilly topography making it naturally resistant to the march of high-rise residential development, the area was now designated a green zone with low-rise public spaces. Later, in 2008, the municipality of Tehran launched an invited competition to design the bridge, teaming up with young designers. The winning scheme goes beyond the bounds of a simple engineering structure to embrace the human dimension of design. The originality of Tabiat Bridge consists in its integration of architecture, structure, landscape and urban design. And this integration extends to its social dimension, as a space that invites all cultural and ethnic communities to use it, without restrictions.

Resting on two tree-shaped supports, the bridge's curved truss branches into multiple decks, offering a variety of places to walk, to gather, to sit, to share cultural activities. One type of bench is used throughout: made of the same material as the paving, these seats seem to rise up directly from the deck, double-curved, wide at one end and narrow at the other, inviting use in many different ways. Likewise, the walking routes wind their way in a non-linear manner, encouraging human encounters and evoking, in a sense, the kind of experience one might traditionally have had walking through a medina. There is an evocation, too, of the tradition of building community and ceremonial bridges in Iran, the prime example of which is Khaju Bridge in Isfahan, constructed under the Safavid dynasty in 1650. A pioneering bridge for its time, it regulated the flow of the river as well as separating carts and horses from pedestrian ways.

Thus, the tradition of pedestrian bridges in Iran is not new, but here this art achieves a new dimension, fully integrating engineering and architecture. All the spaces of Tabiat Bridge are defined by its visible structural elements – its steel trusses. The complexity of the overall structure is underpinned by a rigorous geometry, revealed only when its different layers are seen in elevation and in plan. In this way, the design of the bridge explores an intricate geometry that insinuates a sense of order to generate a place of gathering within an environmentally and ecologically strategic location in Tehran.

1 Interview with Leila Araghian, key architect-designer of Tabiat Bridge, Tehran, 26 April 2016.
2 Farshid Emami, *Civic Visions, National Politics, and International Designs: Three Proposals for a New Urban Center in Tehran (1966–1976),* MSc Thesis in Architecture Studies, MIT, 2011, 13.

LEARNING

How can architecture provide the most appropriate frameworks for knowledge construction? During this cycle of the Award a large number of the shortlisted projects dealt with this topic, an important one for Muslim communities across the globe. But it is worth noting that they adopted vastly different architectural approaches to achieve their goal. The Guelmim School of Technology in Morocco, for example, uses the clarity and order of a modernist approach to produce a series of buildings that through their placement and relation to the landscape create a calm yet vibrant campus. The architecture of this school is in stark contrast to that of the Royal Academy for Nature Conservancy in Jordan, which uses local stone for the construction of a building that fits seamlessly into the surrounding landscape and nature that shape its programme and use.

Issam Fares Institute

Beirut, Lebanon

'This building asserts confidently that we are not a university that stays rooted in time and place; rather we challenge conventional thinking and actively promote change and new ideas', says Peter Dorman, President of the American University of Beirut (AUB), of the Issam Fares Institute, the latest addition to the AUB. In terms of its form, the building is undeniably bold, yet it also displays a sensitivity towards time and place – towards the context, both built and topographical.

The context in this case is the AUB's upper campus, set on a hilltop with views of the Mediterranean. In the immediate vicinity are four historic buildings and some equally venerable – c 150-year-old – Cypress and Ficus trees, as well as one of the most important open areas on the campus, the Green Oval. Responding to the givens of the site, the architects significantly reduced the building's footprint by cantilevering a large part of the structure over the entrance courtyard – a move that also draws the space of the adjacent Green Oval towards the base of the new building. The existing landscape is preserved, including all of the old trees, which form a kind of datum line determining the height of the institute, as is evident from a look at the south facade. Further connections with the landscape are established by the roof terrace, with its expansive views, and by the circulation ramp that snakes smoothly through the trees to the southern entrance on the second floor.

The Issam Fares Institute – a research centre for public policy and international affairs – has a combined surface area of 3,000 m^2, divided into six floors. Its facilities include research spaces and administration offices, seminar and workshop rooms, an auditorium, reading room, recreational lounge and roof terrace. The interiors are divided by walls of partially pigmented glass (though the original idea was for the glazing to be clear, for maximum transparency). The structure is of high-quality in-situ reinforced concrete, in tune with the local construction culture of working with concrete, and particularly fair-faced concrete.

ISSAM FARES INSTITUTE
for Public Policy and International Affairs

Citation

As the last in a series of buildings, the Issam Fares Institute completes the central oval courtyard of the upper campus of American University of Beirut, located on a hill overlooking the Mediterranean. This educational building solves a dense programme within a surprisingly small footprint in a manner that is sensitive to its context. With its contemporary form and the purity of its architectural language the building differentiates itself from its neighbours, though it is not in conflict with the campus and its architecture.

Cantilevering over the courtyard and overlooking the old Cypress and Ficus trees, the building presents an extremely powerful and authentic volumetric structure without obstructing the view from the buildings behind. The building's height, matched with that of the trees and the surrounding structures, serves to strengthen the powerful relationship it creates with its context. Throughout, a fluid planning strategy has turned to advantage the level variances of the site, and a welcoming environment has been created by providing entrances at various levels via ramps that weave through existing trees, in the process becoming part of the landscape themselves.

The building makes a courageous – and at the same time fully respectful – contribution to the multilayered physical environment of this historic and rooted university campus. With its simple, exposed concrete surface and strong volumetric presence, it is an elegant yet unique solution to a complex and special context.

Patron
Issam Fares, Beirut, Lebanon

Client
American University of Beirut (AUB), Beirut, Lebanon:
Peter Dorman, president
Bassem Baroumi, facilities planning and design unit director
Alain Eid, Issam Fares Institute project manager
Tarek Mitri, director of Issam Fares Institute for Public Policy and International Affairs
Rami Khouri, founding director of Issam Fares Institute for Public Policy and International Affairs (2006–2014)

Architect
Zaha Hadid Architects, London, United Kingdom:
Zaha Hadid, Patrik Schumacher, partners
Saleem A Jalil, project manager
Christos Passas, Saleem A Jalil, Graham Modlen, Human Talebi, Brandon Buck, Miya Ushida, project team
Saleem A Jalil, Rokhsana Rakhshani, Teakjin Kim, Ben Holland, Charbel Chagoury, Anas Younes, Fulvio Wirz, Mariagrazia Lanza, Renata Dantas, competition team

Rafik El Khoury & Partners, Beirut, Lebanon:
Rafik El Khoury, principal
Hazar Mansour, Roger Skaff, architects
Georges Sfeir, Maya Charry, Guy Ghosn, structural engineers
Issam Mourad, mechanical engineer
Karim Nammar, electrical engineer
Wassim Sader, acoustics
Zeina Bou Mikhael, contract administrator

Contractor
Kettaneh Construction, Beirut, Lebanon:
Bahzad Choubassi, project director
Elie Awaad, site manager
Sabine Choubassi, Assem Soubra, project coordinators
Georges Saade, mechanical coordinator
Darwesh Haddad, structural engineer

Skylight
Alumco, Choueifat, El Kobeh District, Mount Lebanon

Metal Stairs and Railing
Mechrek Group, Beirut, Lebanon

Mechanical Room Aluminium Louvers
SKAB, Metn, Lebanon

Lifts
Mitsulift Elevating Standards, Metn, Lebanon

Concrete Floor
De-Concrete, Beirut, Lebanon

Gypsum Boards and Paint
Pillar Plan, Beirut, Lebanon

Blinds
Libel, Jal El-Dib, Lebanon

Mechanics, Electrics and Plumbing
CLIMTECH – Climate Technology Electro-Mechanical Contracting, Beirut, Lebanon

Internal Glass-Partition Profiles
Gemino, Padua, Italy
Debbas and Mirodec, Beirut, Lebanon

Tables and Kitchens
DuPont Wilmington, Delaware, USA
HEC, Beirut, Lebanon

Carpet Floor Finish
Pictura, Jdeidet el Metn, Lebanon

Internal Wooden Doors and Kitchens
Awale Awale, Beirut, Lebanon

Internal Steel Doors
Fitzpatrick Sal, Beirut, Lebanon

Project Data
Total site area: 7,000 m^2
Total floor area: 3,000 m^2
Building footprint: 560 m^2
Cost: 8,800,000 USD
Commission: May 2007
Design: July 2007–December 2009
Construction: January 2010–April 2014
Completion: May 2014

Zaha Hadid Architects
Zaha Hadid Architects is a global leader in pioneering research and design investigation. Collaborations with corporations that lead their industries have advanced the practice's diversity and knowledge, whilst the implementation of state-of-the-art technologies has aided the realisation of fluid and dynamic architectural structures. Hadid's vision redefined architecture for the twenty-first century and captured imaginations across the globe. Her legacy endures within the DNA of the design studio she created. Working with office partner Patrik Schumacher for three decades, Zaha Hadid Architects' work arranges form and space into breath-taking spatial compositions.

Zaha Hadid's work of the past 30 years was the subject of critically acclaimed exhibitions at New York's Solomon R Guggenheim Museum in 2006, London's Design Museum in 2007, the Palazzo della Ragione, Padua, Italy in 2009 and the Philadelphia Museum of Art in 2011. Zaha Hadid Architects recently completed the Salerno Maritime Terminal in Italy and Oxford University's Middle East Centre at St Antony's College. The practice is currently working on a diversity of projects worldwide including the new Beijing Airport Terminal Building in Daxing, China, the Sleuk Rith Institute in Phnom Penh, Cambodia, the King Abdullah Financial District Metro Station in Riyadh, Saudi Arabia, and the new Mathematics Gallery at London's Science Museum. Zaha Hadid Architects' portfolio also includes cultural, academic, sporting and infrastructure projects across six continents.

Website
www.zaha-hadid.com

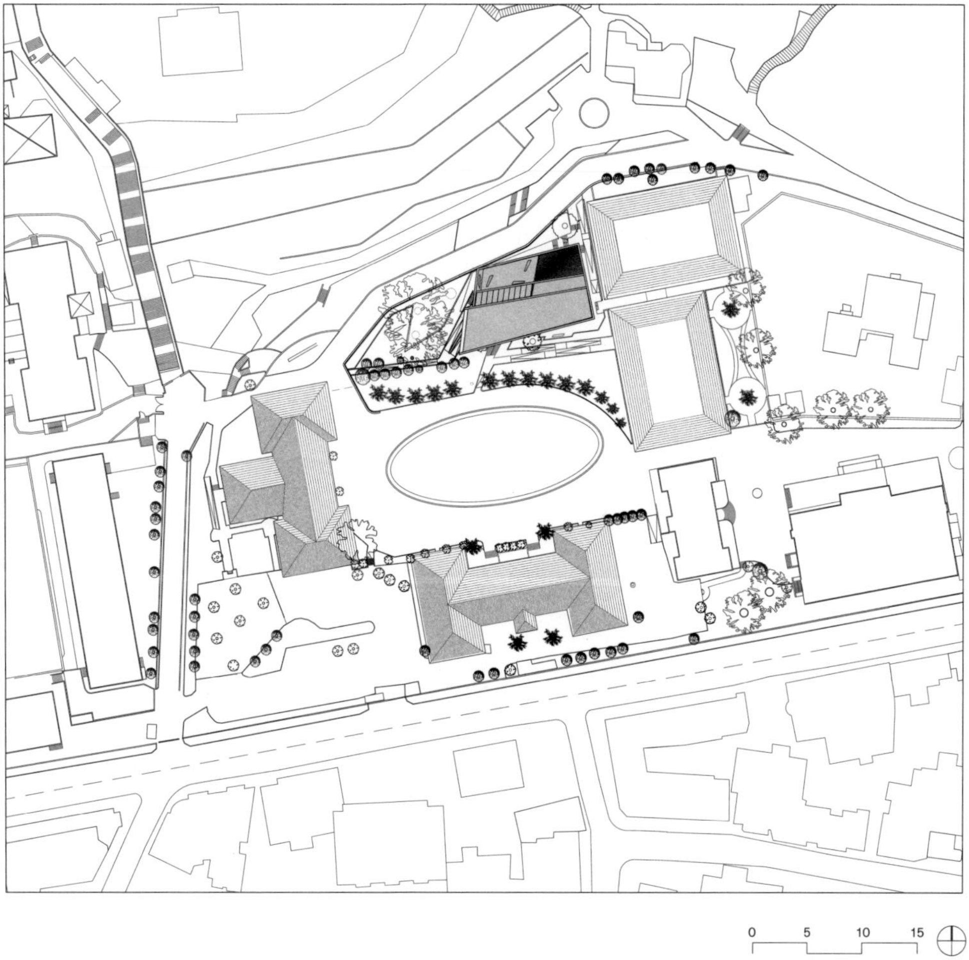
0
5
10
15

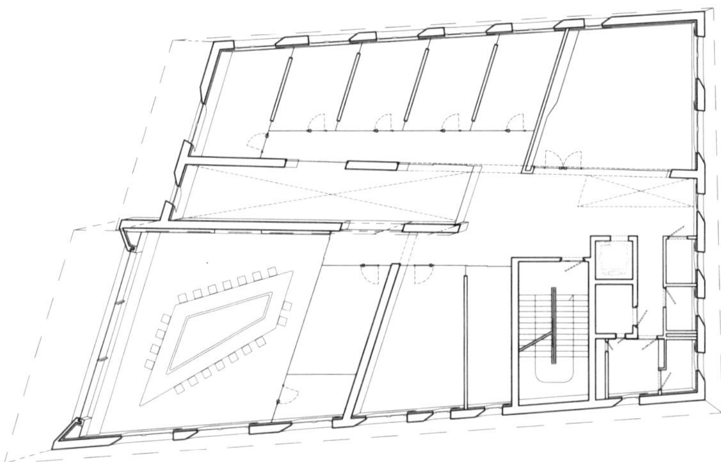

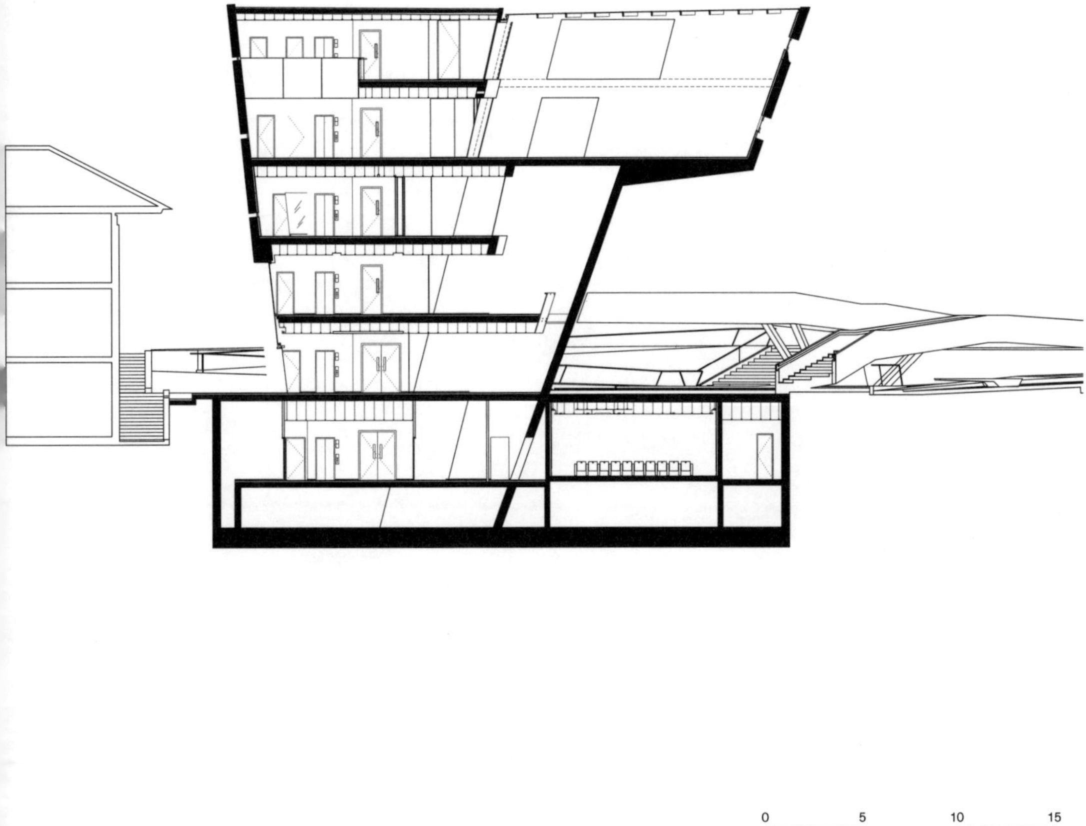
0
5
10
15

PUBLICS

How can the design of buildings, landscapes and public spaces respond to the demands and aspirations of an increasingly multicultural society? One of the challenges facing architecture today is the need to respond to a diversity of conditions and constraints while providing creative spaces for a diversity of users – of publics. Ceuta Public Library is in an autonomous Spanish city on the north coast of Africa. The distance from Spain and the proximity to Morocco, with which it shares a border, affect every aspect of the design and the reception of this building by its users. Equally unusual is the condition of the neighbourhood in Copenhagen that hosts the newly created Superkilen public spaces. Here the architects have worked together with artists and landscape designers to provide a new type of urban park that has the capacity to engage, both physically and emotionally, a culturally diverse group of users.

Superkilen

Copenhagen, Denmark

Superkilen is a kilometre-long urban park located in Nørrebro, a diverse and socially challenged neighbourhood of Copenhagen. Designed by architects BIG – Bjarke Ingels Group, artists Superflex and landscape architects Topotek 1 in collaboration with the local – predominantly Muslim – community, the park takes the historical themes of the universal garden and the amusement park and translates them into a contemporary urban setting. With a healthy dose of irreverence, it sheds light on the positive dimensions of cultural diversity and invites people – young and old – to play.

Superkilen is part of a larger urban renewal plan developed as a partnership between the Municipality of Copenhagen and the private philanthropic association RealDania. Its name refers to the physical constraints of the site, a narrow 'wedge' (*kilen*) extending between two important traffic arteries. The park's pedestrian paths and cycle routes provide better connections between these two roads, while its public lighting creates a greater sense of security – an important consideration in an area historically blighted by crime. Opening up previously hard-to-reach neighbourhoods to the west and east, Superkilen plugs the area back into the infrastructure of the city as a whole.

Colour plays a significant role in the park, which is formally divided into three distinct zones organised around different programmes – Red Square (market/culture/sport), Black Market (urban living room), Green Park (sport/play). Of these, the most visually striking is the Black Market, inspired, according to the architects, by the Lars von Trier film *Dogville* (2003), which uses a minimal stage-like set with white lines on black ground. In the same way, the Black Market could be seen as a stage on which the local residents enact their identities in public space.

These multiple identities are evident in the trees and objects that furnish the park, chosen through an intensive participatory planning process. A swing bench from Baghdad, a star-shaped fountain from Morocco, chess tables from Sofia, basketball hoops from Mogadishu – these are among the park's 108 objects from the 62 home countries of the local inhabitants. Together they form an exhibition of best-practice street furniture from all over the world, and symbolise the residents' ownership of the park.

SIAM
มวยไทย

Citation

Living with people who differ – racially, ethnically, religiously or economically – is the most urgent challenge facing contemporary civil society. At a time of growing global uncertainty and insecurity, it has become fashionable to talk in terms of 'worlds' – the Third World, the Islamic world, the Arab world – as though these occupy a parallel universe, disconnected from the rest and subject to different rules. Superkilen, a new urban park in one of Copenhagen's most diverse and socially challenged neighbourhoods, emphatically rejects this view with a powerful mixture of humour, history and hubris.

It is at once a highly personal yet deeply collective experience, marrying the experiences of migration with an eclectic assembly of displaced objects and innovative landscaping. Here architecture, landscape and art are fused in a truly interdisciplinary manner, providing new opportunities for shared public engagement. A number of different activities – cycling, walking, basketball, hockey – are offered in three separate but connected parks which together form a continuous surface with a marketplace, cafés, retail spaces and open-air gathering spots. In this way, the urban park becomes a public 'stage' where neighbours, strangers and visitors meet. Diversity, as the architects have noted, was not seen as a 'problem' that required a solution, but rather as a tool in a fluid, creative process that allowed the park to become both a powerful marker of identity and a subtle cultural mediator for the residents of this historically challenged neighbourhood.

DeAngelis
Delightfully Different
DONUTS
CITROËN
CIVIC

DONUTS
CITROËN

Clients
RealDania, Copenhagen, Denmark:
Hans Peter Svendler, director
Astrid Bruus Thomsen, programme manager

Copenhagen Municipality, Denmark:
Laura Koch Rotne, project leader & landscape architect
Marion Louw, construction manager
Sanne Gaarde Nielsen, project manager
Thomas Maare, lighting manager
Tina Saaby, city architect

Architect
BIG – Bjarke Ingels Group, Copenhagen, Denmark:
Bjarke Ingels, partner-in-charge
Nanna Gyldholm Møller, Mikkel Marcker Stubgaard, project leaders
Ondrej Tichy, Jonas Lehmann, Rune Hansen, Jan Borgstrøm, Lacin Karaoz, Jonas Barre, Nicklas Antoni Rasch, Gabrielle Nadeau, Jennifer Dahm Petersen, Richard Howis, Fan Zhang, Andreas Castberg, Armen Menendian, Jens Majdal Kaarsholm, Jan Magasanik, project team

Landscape Architect
Topotek 1, Berlin, Germany:
Martin Rein-Cano, Lorenz Dexler, partners
Ole Hartmann, Anna Lundquist, Toni Offenberger, project managers
Katja Steckemetz, Christian Bohne, Karoline Liedtke, Danielle Choi, Dorothee Holzapfel, Lisa Oregioni, Hannes Zander, Marius Hüther, Filippo Tiozzo, David Zimmermann, project team

Art Consultancy
Superflex, Copenhagen, Denmark:
Jakob Fenger, Rasmus Nielsen, Bjørnstjerne Christiansen
Toke Gade Kristiansen, Nikolai Heltoft, Johanne Aarup Hansen, Troels Kahl, project team
Alaa Al-Assadi & Hiba Marwan, Ali Asif & Billal El-Sheikh, Benjamin Heyn-Johnsen & Nicklas Stanley Most, Inga Kristensen & Bent Johannisson, Tove Lerche & Conni Justesen, participation extreme

Engineer
Lemming & Eriksson, Køge, Denmark:
Knud Bay, partner-in-charge
Lars Kofoed, Thomas Kaae-Bodker, project managers
Pia Christiansen, Anne Aaroe Brolund, project team

General Contractor
Aarsleff, Åbyhøj, Denmark:
Mads Hellmers, head of projects
Finn Pedersen, president

Kilebestyrelsen, Local Governance Board involved in selection of objects
Andreas Nøhr, Arsalan Alvi, Besarm Rakipi, Brigitte Kabel, Claus Raasted, Klaus Lorentzen, Samar Subhie, Martin Wåhlin, Mikkel J. Clausen, Mohammed A. Rasmussen, Uzma Ahmed Andersen, Salim El-Chahabi, Troels Glismann, Valdemar Meehrsohn Stauning, Copenhagen, Denmark

Project Data
Total area: 33,000 m^2
Total length: 750 m
Cost: 8,879,000 USD
Commission: June 2008
Design: January 2009–February 2010
Construction: August 2010–June 2012
Completion: June 2012

Bjarke Ingels
Bjarke Ingels started BIG – Bjarke Ingels Group in 2005 after co-founding PLOT Architects in 2001 and working at the Office of Metropolitan Architecture in Rotterdam, The Netherlands. Through a series of award-winning design projects and buildings, Bjarke has developed a reputation for designing buildings that are as programmatically and technically innovative as they are cost- and resource-conscious. He has received numerous awards and honours, including the Danish Crown Prince's Culture Prize in 2011, the Golden Lion at the Venice Biennale in 2004, and the Urban Land Institute (ULI) Award for Excellence in 2009. In 2011, the Wall Street Journal awarded him the Architectural Innovator of the Year Award and, in 2016, Time Magazine named Bjarke one of the 100 most influential people in the world today.

Martin Rein-Cano
Martin Rein-Cano was born in Buenos Aires in 1967. He studied art history at Frankfurt University and landscape architecture at the Technical Universities of Hannover and Karlsruhe. After working in the office of Peter Walker and Martha Schwartz in San Francisco, in 1996 he founded Topotek 1, a practice which partakes in a wide variety of international projects and has achieved first prize in various competitions. Several professional books and articles have been published exclusively on his work, which has been honoured with many awards and prizes. Martin Rein-Cano has been appointed as a guest professor in different academic institutions in Europe and North America, such as the University of Pennsylvania and Harvard University. Presently he is teaching at the Dessau Institute for Architecture. He frequently lectures at internationally renowned universities and cultural institutions and regularly serves on competition juries.

Superflex
Superflex is an artist group that was founded in 1993 by Bjørnstjerne Christiansen, Jakob Fenger and Rasmus Nielsen. Their works, which challenge power structures and relate to economics, copyright law and self-organisation, are described by Superflex as tools, as proposals that invite people to participate in the development of experimental models to alter given structures and conditions. Superflex works within, and outside of, traditional art contexts. The group collaborates with architects, designers, engineers, businesses and marketers on tools which have the potential for social or economic change.

Website
www.big.dk
www.topotek1.de
www.superflex.net

0 5 10 15

Superkilen – A Playground for Pluralism

Azra Akšamija

Do you remember the first time you ate food from another culture? At first, it might have seemed strange, but the more you were exposed to it – the more you explored the menu – the more you developed a taste for it. Similar to our cultural adjustment to a foreign cuisine, a walk through Copenhagen's kilometre-long Superkilen park allows visitors to experience something new by encountering fragments of other cultures. Seeing and using alien objects on a daily basis gradually transforms perceptions, turning an 'exotic' culture into a culture that is part of everyday life.

A joint effort of three teams – the architectural office BIG – Bjarke Ingels Group), landscape architects Topotek 1 and the artist group Superflex – Superkilen deploys a bold and innovative design to provide an enjoyable space for a multicultural context. More than that, it points to new ways in which architecture can shape the convergence between peoples, countering narratives of cultural misrepresentation with an argument in favour of diversity.

The discussion around architecture and pluralism in relation to Islam is still predominantly framed in terms of religious space. And certainly, the proliferation of mosques and Islamic cemeteries in Europe, with their culturally hybrid designs, bears witness to the positive dynamics of cultural and religious diversification, signalling that many Muslims feel at home in the region. Yet this programmatic focus is problematic for two reasons. First, religious architecture cannot sufficiently account for the various cultural and secular needs of the very heterogeneous Muslim communities in Europe. Second, the concern for the advancement of pluralism in Europe is larger than the concern for the representation of Islam. Europe's demographic landscape is changing due to the movement of many other migrant groups. In this context the scope of our architectural explorations needs to be broadened to find ways of giving these groups better access to public space and, with this, greater visibility in the cities which we all share. This is what Superkilen achieves in Nørrebro, the most culturally diverse and socially challenged neighbourhood of Copenhagen.

Today more than half the residents of Nørrebro, that is some 10,745 people, come from countries with a Muslim majority, such as Bosnia-Herzegovina, Turkey, Somalia, Morocco, Iran, Iraq, Jordan, Lebanon, Pakistan and Syria. This cultural diversity is historically deeply rooted in the neighbourhood, as is its other defining characteristic – its capacity for unrest triggered by social and cultural friction. A succession of protests and riots over the past 150 years created a negative image of Nørrebro, reinforced more recently by problems related to violent crime, gang activity and a lack of cultural integration – a disconnect mirrored in the area's lack of linkages with the infrastructure of the city as a whole. In the background to the project's inception we also find the so-called cartoons controversy that broke out in 2005 after the *Jyllands-Posten* newspaper published 12 caricatures of the Prophet Muhammad. The cartoons provoked protests worldwide but in Nørrebro, specifically, they gave rise to vandalism, flag-burning and violent clashes between the police and frustrated youths.

Issues of integration and the coexistence of different cultures were near the top, then, of the list of priorities for the project for the regeneration of Nørrebro initiated and developed by the Municipality of Copenhagen and RealDania, a private philanthropic association. As part of this larger project, Superkilen was designed for a number of different functions. First, it connects Nørrebro to the surrounding neighbourhoods, facilitating safe and transparent pedestrian and cyclist transit with paths designed specifically for this purpose. Second, as a public park, it provides for a variety of outdoor activities such as cultural events, leisure and sport. Third, it functions as an exhibition of the neighbourhood's cultural diversity. All three dimensions have made Superkilen one of the most popular and best-functioning public spaces in the city of Copenhagen.

Among its many qualities, four aspects of the project may be highlighted for their contribution to the discourse on the architecture of pluralism in Europe: inclusive design, cultural mobility, branding and play.

Inclusive Design

Superkilen's extraordinary aesthetic is defined by the creation of three formally distinct zones – the Red Square, the Black Market and Green Park – furnished with a diverse array of urban objects 'sampled' from all over the world. Local inhabitants were invited to propose specific city objects – benches, playground equipment, lamps, bins, trees, etc – from another country, which could either be their own homeland, or a place they had travelled to. The collecting of objects was intended to reflect the culturally diverse landscape of Nørrebro while also promoting a sense of ownership. The arrangement of selected objects was curated by the project architects and artists, resulting in an exhibition of 'best-practice' urban furniture. A special app was developed to give visitors more detailed information about the objects.

The design of Superkilen is site-specific, yet the core approach is certainly applicable to the making of other public spaces. Rather than attempting to determine every component of the design, the architects and artists tapped into local intelligence, recognising and validating the expertise of the residents as specialists in their own culture and identity. Repeatedly, through an outreach exercise involving a wide array of communication channels, residents were invited to articulate their needs, with the designers taking on the role of curators, mediators and motivators in a collective effort of creating public space. While the majority of Nørrebro's residents have an Islamic and/or Middle Eastern background, the design does not favour a single religious or ethnic group. Rather, cultural representation in the park promotes the notion of diversity through self-representation.

An inventive aspect of the design process was the so-called 'Participation Extreme' approach developed by Superflex as a way of including the less vocal and less dominant members of the community. The artists asked groups of youths and elderly people, 'If you could choose anything from anywhere you wanted, what would you like to see in the park?', and then travelled with residents to five of the proposed sites – Thailand, Spain, Palestine, USA and Jamaica – to find these objects. In this way, they gave voice to the needs and desires of those who are usually left out of participatory planning processes.

Cultural Mobility

Alongside its inclusive design, Superkilen gives form to pluralism by integrating the notion of migration into the design and implementation process. The trees in the park, for example, symbolise the various aspects of migration through their transplantation and acculturation to local climatic and soil conditions. Just like the migrants in Nørrebro, Superkilen's trees come from different parts of the world. Species from the Islamic world – the Cedars native to Lebanon or to the Atlas Mountains of Algeria and Morocco – are planted side by side with species such as the European Larch, native to central Europe; Nothofagus antarctica, a variety of Beech native to Andean regions; or the Ginko, native to China. Yet the notion of the trees' origins is not that clear-cut: although native to different parts of the world, most of the specimens were transplanted from nurseries in Northern Germany or Denmark. In this way, the concept probes the defining parameters of cultural or national origins.

The concept of a mini world's fair of urban furniture and vegetation also points to the global flows of culture, as well as the many forms of translations to a local context. The objects installed in the park were either purchased from catalogues or reproduced from photographs – though in many cases the photos did not reveal much detail about the objects' size or composition and the construction schemes had to be invented. Elsewhere, the design of the park's furniture had to be modified to conform to Danish safety standards. There were also instances of things getting 'lost in translation', as in the case of the Octopus built by local workers in tandem with the Japanese craftsmen who spent a month in Copenhagen, building the creature on site. As inspirations are imported from one context to another, this process revealed the creative dimensions of cultural mobility: the construction of objects was not so much a replication as an invention of new cultural forms.

In the realisation of some of the Participation Extreme projects, the notion of cultural mobility took on a highly symbolic dimension. 'Soil from Palestine', for example, is just that: soil brought mostly from the occupied Golan Heights but also from East Jerusalem, from Ramallah, from the West Bank. This symbolically charged proposal came from two teenage girls, Hiba and Alaa, residents of Nørrebro. While they had never been to Palestine and only knew about their homeland through stories, both of them identified as Palestinian. The Participation Extreme project made it possible for them to visit Palestine and to bring back Palestinian soil. When the imported red soil was first distributed on top of the little hill on the Black Market, it stood in high contrast to the local sandy brown earth. Over time, however, the two soils have merged with one another – a symbolic reference to the process of migration, cultural integration and the blending of identities. In its mixing and blending of different soils, this project reflects the fears of losing one's own cultural identity, but also the possibility of belonging to more than one place and culture.

Branding

From the aesthetic perspective, colour and materials play an important role in articulating the formal and symbolic qualities of the park. The red of the Red Square, for example, can be interpreted at a variety of scales – from a domestic rug with furniture, to a Danish flag with the red symbolising Denmark's multinational soil that unifies inhabitants of various backgrounds. In formal terms, however, perhaps the most visually striking part of the park is the Black Market, with its black asphalt and its white stripes which direct the movement of people around the site. This aspect of the design was inspired by the Lars von Trier film *Dogville* (2003), which uses a minimal stage-like set with white lines on black ground to demarcate scenes. In a similar way, the Black Market also reads like a stage on which residents can publicly enact their identities.

Initially resisted by a portion of the residents who were hoping for a more traditional park design, the bold colours and unusual materials were important tools in the rebranding of the neighbourhood, helping to establish a once notorious area as a regular feature in lists of the 'top ten attractions to visit in Copenhagen'. Today, the red, black and green have become important markers of identity for Nørrebro as a whole, as attested by a recent discussion regarding the replacement of surfaces on the Red Square, when the majority of residents made it clear that the new surfaces had also to be red. In turn, the black and white stripes of the Black Market have appeared as the backdrop to numerous fashion and advertising campaigns. The popularity of the branding is such that you can even get an iPhone case featuring a photograph of a skater over the stripes.

Play

The fourth dimension of Superkilen's important contribution to the architecture of pluralism relates to the way in which its aesthetic and programmatic components work together in the service of cultural representation. The landscaping of Superkilen constitutes a contemporary urban hybrid of two historical themes in landscape architecture – the universal garden and the amusement park. Purposefully using exoticism to embrace symbols of various identities, the park makes everyone feel both a bit alien and a bit at home. The programme, a kind of 'playground for adults', provides infrastructure for people of various cultural backgrounds and age groups to come together without any sense of forced integration. For example, two of the most visited and used objects in the park, the Swing Bench from Baghdad and the Octopus from Tokyo, bring Muslims and non-Muslims into close proximity. While the children are playing, their parents interact, striking up conversations.

The project is also courageous and unique in the way it simultaneously embraces and disarms cultural stereotypes. The Neon Sign from Doha, Qatar, for example, seemingly flags the Black Market with an Islamic symbol – that of the crescent and a star. But a closer look reveals that the star is not quite what it seems: in fact, this sign was copied from a dental clinic in Doha, where a local dentist enterprisingly replaced the star with the shape of a molar tooth as a way of advertising his business. This humorous take on a potent religious and cultural symbol within the context of an Islamic country at once challenges stereotypes and opens up possibilities for play.

The notion of play was also utilised to counter crime. Superkilen acknowledges the need to recognise groups that might be prone to violence and to give them space and visibility, for example, in the Thai Boxing Ring or the curved surfaces attractive to skaters, which channel young men's energies into sport and competition. Such an approach is not about an attempt to control or avoid conflict. The principle here is that violence can be more dangerous when it is hidden in a dark park than when it is staged and exposed in a specially designated space, such as the boxing ring. While public space needs to accommodate social and cultural tension to a certain degree, a successful design also needs to articulate a balance between the dangerous and the constructive aspects of this tension – something that Superkilen achieves through both aesthetic and programmatic means.

Born out of an intense engagement with its users, Superkilen has introduced new aesthetic and critical dimensions to participatory design, setting new standards for the creation of public space. The notion of inclusive design is also reflected in the very constellation of the project team. Combining humour with respect and cultural sensitivity, Superkilen demonstrates the agency of architecture, art and landscape design in maintaining a healthy public space – a space where one can encounter things that one either does not know about, or agree with. The contribution of the park towards promoting an inclusive and heterogeneous society is of particular importance at a time when European society is becoming increasingly conservative and unfortunately more hostile towards its Muslim minorities and migrant groups. Perhaps the best summary of the larger lesson to be taken from Superkilen lies in the calligraphic inscriptions on the park benches from Iran: 'A good city can not be found, you have to build it!'

SHORTLISTED PROJECTS

Bunateka Libraries

Various locations, Kosovo

The majority of schools in rural Kosovo share one feature in common: they are without libraries. This project aspires to help build knowledge in a new generation by providing reading resources in an environment that children would find both enjoyable and stimulating. The design concept, though simple, takes many issues into consideration. Bunatekas are freestanding, so they do not take up space in existing structures. The materials used are standard and widely available. Construction can take as little as three weeks. Louvers allow for natural ventilation and, where possible, the buildings are sited under trees for shade. Removed in this way from the confines of the classroom, the world of books becomes ensconced in the place of adventure and play.

Each virtually identical structure is a 4 m × 6 m × 3 m box of timber and glass on a concrete foundation, with interior furniture and shelving made from wood. The style is contemporary, while reminiscent of the *majlis* (sitting rooms) of traditional houses in the region. So far eight Bunatekas have been built. The project is partly funded by the Swiss and the Norwegian embassies in Prishtina. Bujar Nrecaj, the architect who developed the concept, grew up in rural Kosovo – then a province of a disintegrating Yugoslavia – before moving to Switzerland at the age of 12.

Perhaps unsurprisingly, Bunatekas have become neighbourhood hubs for more than schoolchildren. Books are donated by community members to enhance the school's offerings. The thoughtful design of these one-room libraries enables fluid perceptual movement from exterior yards to inviting interiors, fostering connections between the greenery outside, the people inside, and the imaginary spaces within books and minds.

The architectural value of this project lies in its conceptual simplicity. Beyond their role as spaces of learning, Bunatekas are also infrastructural devices that can enhance both the spatial and the educational quality of schools across the country.

bunateka

Locations
Lutogllavë, Sferkë, Bajgorë, Mohlan, Drenoc, Celinë, Bostan, Lubinjë e Epërme

Clients
Royal Embassy of Norway, Prishtina, Kosovo:
Sverre Johan Kvale, ambassador

Swiss Embassy, Prishtina, Kosovo

Architect
bnarchitects, Prizen, Kosovo:
Bujar Nrecaj, principal

Concept Development
Naser Morina, University of Zürich, Switzerland

Contractor
Jetoj SH.P.K., Prizren, Kosovo

Local Partners
Directorates of Education in Kosovo: Prizren, Klina, Mitrovica, Suharekë, Deçan, Rahovec, Novoberde

Project Data
Built area: 24 m^2 per library
Total cost: 226,200 USD
Cost per library: 28,200 USD
Design: November 2007–May 2008
Construction: May 2009–April 2012
Completion: 2012

Bujar Nrecaj
Bujar Nrecaj is an architect who believes that the quality of the built environment is a crucial component of people's lives and that it is enhanced by architecture derived from a very specific context – a 'place architecture'. In the early 1990s he left his home village, Lutogllavë in the municipality of Prizren, to emigrate to Switzerland, where he grew up, completed his architectural studies and worked for different architectural offices on projects such as the Novartis Campus laboratory building by Eduardo Souto de Moura. Kosovo's declaration of independence in 2008 inspired him to return to Kosovo with a cause – to give rural children greater access to books. He founded his own architectural office, bnarchitects, to practise an architecture that is derived from a very specific context and for specific people – with the goal of creating a meaningful built environment. Concurrently with the Bunateka libraries, he has also built also the very unique multi-ethnic Hotel Graçanica near Prishtina, a Swiss investment with Roma partners. At the moment Bujar Nrecaj is living in Switzerland again and working on an idea to expand the Bunatekas around the world to places where young people do not have proper access to books.

Website
www.bnarchitects.com

Bajgorë
Bostan
Sferkë
Drenoc
Mohlan
Celinë
Lutogllavë
Lubine e Eperme

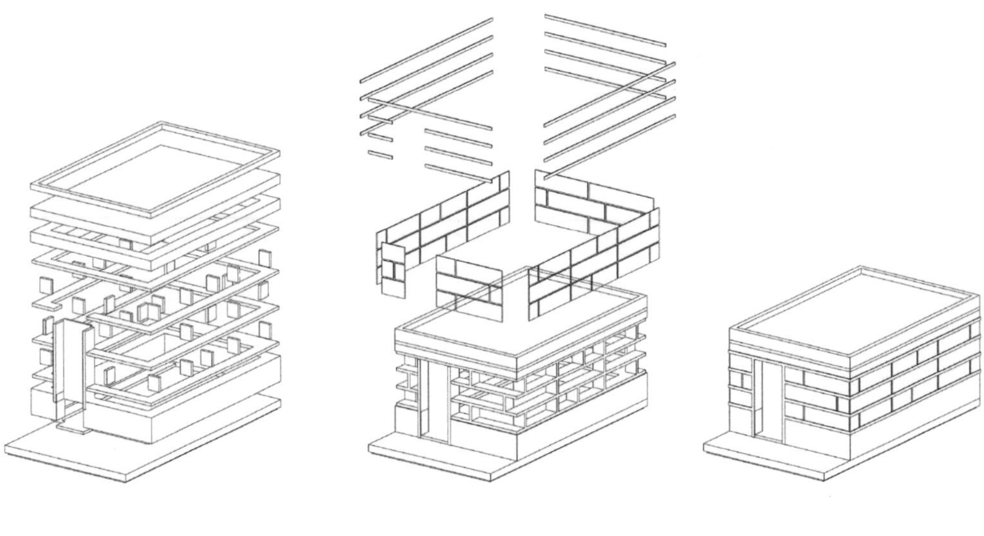

New Power Station

Baku, Azerbaijan

The two connected buildings of the New Power Station sit near their inspiration, one of the oldest power stations in Baku. The original brief included the demolition of the original late-nineteenth century limestone structures, but the architect advocated their preservation, arguing for their historical and aesthetic importance. Together, the structures create a transformed space in which the new is in dialogue with the existing, helping to preserve the collective memory of the industrial legacy of the site.

The New Power Station functions as an important component in the city's cultural revitalisation efforts. The larger building of the two offers a flexible event space and restaurant, the smaller one is a vibrant youth-centred jazz club. Jazz has deep roots in Azerbaijan, where traditional musical forms are characterised by improvisation. Local jazz bands were performing in Baku in the early 1900s and it remained popular even when banned by the Soviet regime. The club is imagined as a space where jazz music can be played and cultivated, making an important contribution to the local and national music scene.

The buildings are located on the Bay of Baku, a natural harbour once lined by shipyards and warehouses. They are part of a larger site, the National Flag Square, within the city's expanding waterfront green zone. The courtyard forms an open space between the new and old power stations, connecting the former industrial site with its surroundings and offering a flexible space that the architect imagines could be used as an open-air market.

An enclosed bridge links the two simple, geometric structures. Their form mimics that of the older power station, while their facades, clad in laminated timber and zinc, are distinctly contemporary in design. The architecture of the New Power Station pays homage, both formally and materially, to an older tradition of industrial buildings without sharing their functional use.

ELEKTRA
EVENTS HALL

Client
Pasha Construction, Baku, Azerbaijan:
Jalal Pashayev, managing director
Javad Marandi, managing partner

Architects
Erginoğlu & Çalışlar Architects, Istanbul, Turkey:
Hasan Çalışlar, Kerem Erginoğlu, principals
Fatih Kariptaş, Zeynep Şenkaynağı, Serhat Özkan, Sezen Bilge, İdil Yücel, Füsun Seçer Kariptaş, project team

Pasha Construction, Baku, Azerbaijan:
Dinçer Filiz, senior project manager
Didem Dengiz Karasu, site and project manager
Ceyda Ay, Türkan Kahveci, site manager team
Murat Işik, senior MEP manager
Muharrem Uysal, lead MEP engineer
Kenan Huseynov, construction engineer
Ceyda Ay, site architect
Vasif Yagubov, mechanical engineer
Zaur Huseynov, electric engineer
Agil Rahimov, survey engineer
Halil Yağiz, site supervisor
Rashad Ashrafov, project procurement specialist
Bahruz Mahmudov, site administrator

Reinforced Concrete
Neftyoltikintitamir ASC, Baku, Azerbaijan

Steel Structure
Samqayit Polad Konstruksiya-Qurastirma ASC, Baku, Azerbaijan

Water Insulation
Xansaray MMC, Baku, Azerbaijan

Envelope Works
Sinerji İnşaat Mimarlık Müşavirlik Taah San ve Tic AŞ, Istanbul, Turkey

Mechanical and Electrical Engineering
Çağla Group, Istanbul, Turkey
D&T, Istanbul, Turkey

Fibre Concrete Works Contractor
Silkway Fibrobeton, Baku, Azerbaijan

Masonry
Jamaleddin Abdulkerimov, Baku, Azerbaijan

Structural Project
Ural Muhendislik Engineering, Ankara, Turkey

Lighting Consultant
Lighting Design Collective, Madrid, Spain

Interior Design
Blue Sky Hospitality (Jazz Club), London, England
Erginoğlu & Çalışlar (Events Hall), Istanbul, Turkey

Acoustic Consultant
Sandy Brown Associates, London, England

Project Data
Site area: 10,000 m^2
Built area: 8,500 m^2
Ground floor area: 2,208 m^2
Cost: 24,000,000 USD
Commission: September 2011
Design: September 2011–March 2012
Construction: March 2012–November 2013
Occupancy: January 2014

Erginoğlu & Çalışlar Architects
Erginoğlu & Çalışlar Architects is an Istanbul-based, independent studio of architects founded in 1993 by Hasan Çalışlar and Kerem Erginoğlu. The 'E&C Team' specialises in urban planning, architecture and interior design projects, together with providing assistance for planning applications.

The ethos of the company is to view each project within its individual context and contribute to it through innovative architectural solutions. It has evolved to adopt a circumstantial architectural approach with careful consideration to social impact and participatory design. The studio has vast experience gained through successful completion of a wide variety of both national and international projects on a range of scales.

Erginoğlu & Çalışlar Architects have won many prizes and awards for their innovative projects. These include: the Building Award for the Tarsus Sev Elementary School Campus project in the National Architecture Awards of 2016; the New & Old Award for the Salt Repository-Medina Turgul DDB Headquarters at the World Architecture Festival 2010; the Building Award for the Turkcell Teknoloji Research and Development Building and the Preservation-Revitalisation Award for the Salt Repository – Medina Turgul DDB in the National Architecture Awards of 2010; first prize in the invited competition for Tarsus Sev Elementary School Campus in 2009; fourth prize in the international competition for the Turkish Embassy in Berlin in 2007; an AMV Young Architects Award in 2004; and the Building Award for the Military School Swimming Pool Complex in the National Architecture Awards of 2000.

In addition to architecture and design services, the partners also lecture and organise architectural workshops in universities across Turkey.

Website
www.ecarch.com

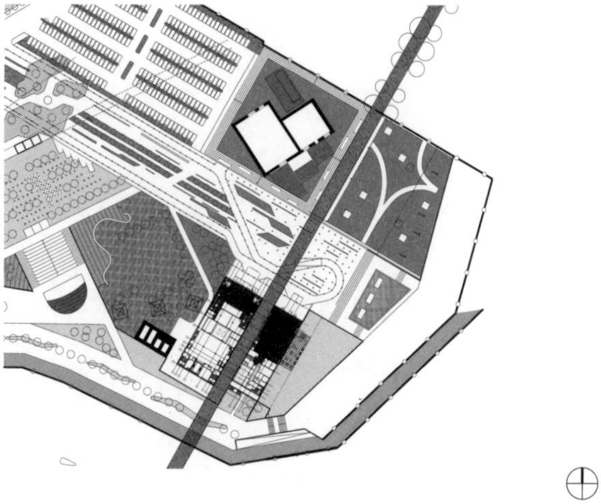

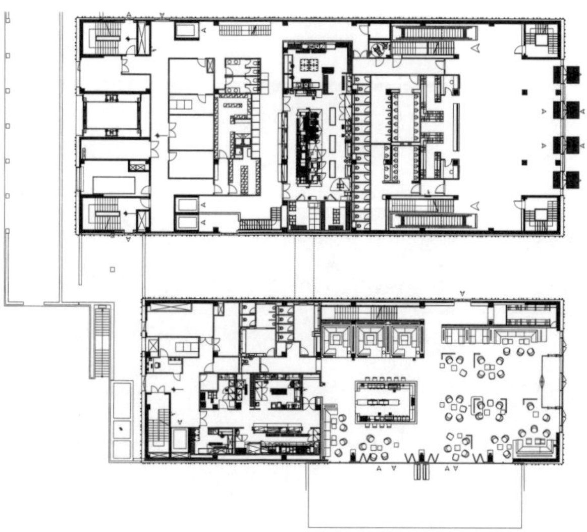

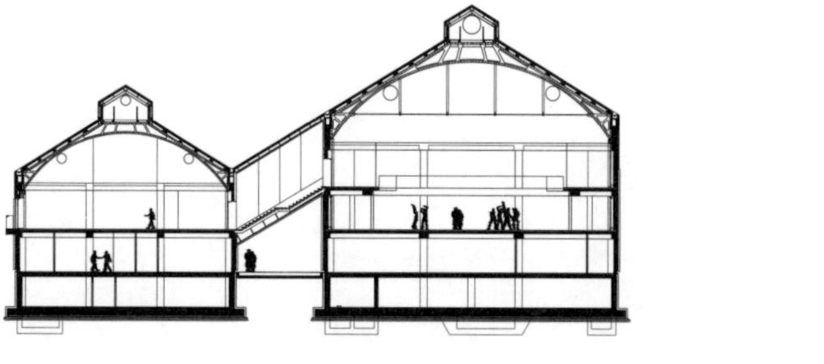
0 5 10 15

The Place of Culture, Heritage and Architecture in an Urban Planet

Francesco Bandarin

Every 20 years the United Nations convenes a summit to examine the state of the urban world. The agenda of Habitat III, held in Quito, Ecuador, in 2016, makes it clear that great challenges lie ahead. Over the next two decades the processes of urbanisation will continue to pick up pace, especially in Asia and Africa, resulting in a massive expansion of both intermediate urban centres and metropolitan areas – in short, defining Earth as an urban planet. Yet the physical environments that are being created to shelter these hundreds of millions of new city-dwellers are shaped by industrial and commercial enterprises more concerned with volume and quantity than with space and quality. The outcome? Conglomerates of concrete and steel, inhuman places, prone to social degradation and violence.

If we look to history, to the postwar period, we can see this has happened before. In regions such as Western and Eastern Europe and the Americas, strong processes of urban migration – different from the current ones in scale, but not in speed – prompted the creation of immense urban peripheries. Only in a few cases, and only with the full passage of time, did these become something like liveable spaces. In many other parts of the world, endless slums are the default living environments for the urbanised masses.

While we are still struggling to cope with the urbanisation processes that dominated the second part of the twentieth century, the developments that we are witnessing now will have a far greater impact still, affecting the lives of billions of people. If today's urban population is estimated at 54 per cent of the total, that figure will reach 70 per cent by the middle of the century. By then, it is projected that some 2.3 billion people will be living in urban areas in the developing world. Metropolitan conurbations are multiplying: within 15 years, there will be 41 cities with a population of more than 10 million. The fastest growth, however, will be in medium-sized towns and cities of 500,000 to 1 million inhabitants, mostly located in Africa and Asia. The Islamic world, then, will be placed at the centre of this tectonic shift.

How can these processes be humanised? Government plans are mainly concerned with primary needs. At most, they provide the basic infrastructures for transport, water and sanitation, as we can see in the burgeoning metropolises of Asia, Africa, Latin America. Little thought is given to the only factor that can make a difference: culture.

Making a place for culture means understanding the shapes and needs of communities, respecting people's identities and expressions, protecting their physical environments. Humanised, liveable cities – that is what culture, heritage and architecture can offer to the urbanising planet.

A culture-based approach to urban sustainability needs above all to value what comes from the people. No top-down, centralised urban planning system has ever been able to understand the needs of communities or to integrate the cultural dimension of projects into the development of the city as a whole. If governments wish to ensure the long-term success and sustainability of their investments in the city, they need to privilege dialogue and interaction with local communities, and adapt schemes and plans to local needs. This is the issue highlighted by the preparatory work for the Habitat III conference, and perhaps the main message to come out of this collective reflection on the future of the urban planet.

Listening to the people means understanding and valuing their culture – the intangible heritage that infuses their everyday life. A working partnership based on these principles can help to shape people-centred, affordable, sustainable environments.

The richness and the potential of traditional architectural knowledge is part of the culture of communities that must be valued and protected. Earthen and wooden architecture, for instance, constitutes a fundamental resource for the creation of sustainable and harmonious physical environments. Traditional knowledge has also contributed towards making urban areas more resilient in the face of natural disasters – an issue of increasing relevance to the future of our cities.

The urban heritage may only make up a small part of the physical environment of a modern city, yet it can still represent its core and its soul. Historic environments are invaluable, not only as places where people find their identity, but also as guides for modern planners, offering models for the design of structures and places that are able to withstand the test of time and, through this, be embraced as part of the heritage of a people, even as one culture succeeds another, in the flow of history.

Nowhere is the importance of a heritage-based approach more evident than in the design of public spaces, where cultures meet and the identities of communities coalesce. Public spaces also provide a means of connecting culture and nature, in places where ecosystems and human uses interact.

From ample experience, we know that heritage areas have the potential to drive the economic processes linked to tourism and to the development of the creative sector – a decisive element in the new urban economies, encompassing fields as diverse as design, the visual and performing arts, the media, food and fashion.

Architecture and urban design are key tools for these transformations. As socially oriented practices, they have the potential to respond to the demands of the urban century. They can give appropriate answers to the challenges of providing affordable housing, inclusive public spaces and harmonious environments. They can create beauty and a sense of belonging; they can mitigate emergencies.

Faced with climate change, vulnerability to natural disasters, expanding conflicts, the displacement of millions of people and increasing migratory flows, our urban planet needs answers that only culture, heritage and architecture can provide.

Thread Cultural Centre

Sinthian, Senegal

Thread is a cultural centre and artists' residency in a remote village in south-east Senegal. Located next to a health centre, its entire operations speak of a notion of 'culture' that goes beyond the arts to encompass the whole life of the community, supporting physical well-being, education, agriculture and entrepreneurship.

Built with local materials and limited resources, the centre provides for a multiplicity of uses. A 1000 m^2 rainwater-harvesting roof defines a large flexible space – with both open and closed areas – and two residences for visiting artists from both Senegal and abroad. Four bungalows set apart from the main building accommodate Thread's permanent staff.

The load-bearing masonry construction consists of concrete columns and beams infilled with compressed earth blocks. All vertical surfaces are plastered and painted white. The perforated ventilation walls, with their strong, textural bas-relief, add a further aesthetic dimension – as does the beautifully articulated floor, which embeds broken shards of tiles (cast-offs from a local factory) in a cement screed. The roof consists of a primary structure of metal with secondary wooden rafters and bamboo purlins supporting the thatch.

The sinuous, undulating roof is designed as a 'parametric transformation' of the traditional pitched roofs of the impluvium houses in the Casamance region of southwest Senegal. Its curving geometry inscribes two elliptical courtyards where rainwater is collected and channelled into two ditches, each leading to a 570 m^3 reservoir. This water is used to irrigate vegetable crops, supplementing the villagers' largely rice-based diet.

With its intrinsic potential to operate as an open platform, the space under the roof does not specify modes of use but allows for experimentation, doubling – amongst other guises – as an extension of the health centre, as a setting for workshops in gardening and farming techniques, as a space to study in the afternoon, as a stage for performance and for artistic expression. This is culture, not as a luxury for a few, but as a universal right for all.

Patron
Le Korsa and the Josef and Anni Albers Foundation, New York, USA:
Nicholas Fox Weber, executive director

Client
Thread, Sinthian, Senegal:
Nick Murphy, director
Moussa Diogoye Sene, general manager
Habib Dieye, coordinator of agricultural projects
Augustin Diouf, assistant coordinator of agricultural projects
Brian Harris, agricultural and cultural coordinator

Architect
Toshiko Mori Architect, New York, USA:
Toshiko Mori, principal
Jordan MacTavish, project architect

Structural Engineer
Schlaich Bergermann and Partner, Stuttgart, Germany:
Michael Stein, managing director

General Contractor
Maison médicale mutualiste de Sinthian, Senegal:
Magueye Ba, director and general contractor

Mason
Pepe Ndiaye, Sinthian, Senegal

Brickwork
Elhadjil Kante, Sinthian, Senegal

Roof Constructor
Gregoire Bienquench, Sinthian, Senegal

Project Data
Total built area: 1,000 m^2
Cost: 146,000 USD
Commission: 2012
Design: January 2013–November 2013
Construction: December 2013–February 2015
Completion: February 2015

Toshiko Mori
Toshiko Mori Architect (TMA) is known for over 30 years of innovative and influential work in a diverse body of projects that have received numerous design awards. Mori's intelligent approach to ecologically sensitive siting strategies, historical context and innovative use of materials reflects a creative integration of design and technology. Her designs demonstrate a thoughtful sensitivity to detail and involve extensive research into the site conditions and surrounding context. The work of TMA combines a strong conceptual and theoretical approach with a thorough study of programmatic needs and practical conditions to achieve a design that is both spatially compelling and pragmatically responsive.

Toshiko Mori Architect has worked on a broad range of programmes including urban, civic, institutional, cultural, residential, museum and exhibition design. Recent work includes New York City theatre, library and museum projects, the Hudson Yard Park and Boulevard, and a park visitor centre in the Bronx. Mori designed institutional projects for Brown University and Syracuse University, and is included on the design team for New York University's strategic master plan. The firm was selected twice for the New York City's Department of Design and Construction's Design and Construction Excellence programme, and won four competitions for the programme's public and urban infrastructure projects. TMA was also recently selected as the architect of a laboratory building for Novartis' extended Cambridge campus.

Toshiko Mori Architect continues to engage in an architecture of material exploration, technological invention and theoretical provocation.

Website
www.tmarch.com
www.thread-senegal.org

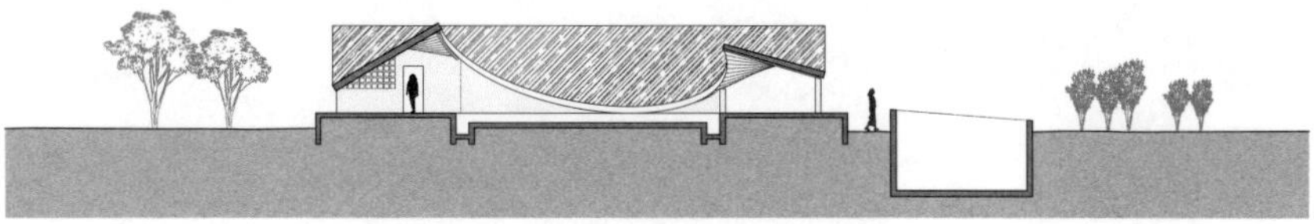

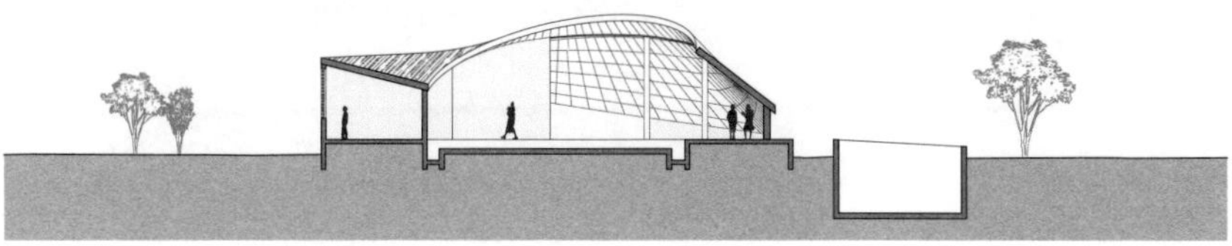

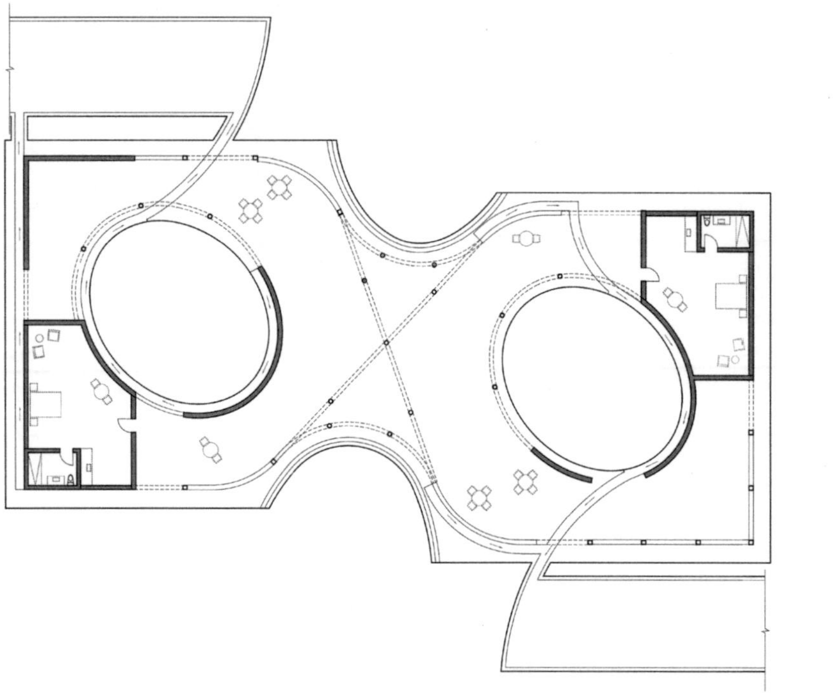
0
5
10
15

The 'Development' Bind

Lesley Lokko

Bind. *Noun.*
A problematical situation, eg 'He is in a political bind over the trade issue.'
Synonyms: predicament, awkward situation, quandary, dilemma, plight, cleft stick, mess, quagmire.[1]

In 2005 the Kenyan writer Binyavanga Wainaina published a controversial essay, 'How To Write About Africa'. It remains the most forwarded article in the history of *Granta* magazine. With an uneasy combination of laugh-out-loud satire and biting sarcasm, Wainaina offers a number of tips for would-be writers: 'always use the word "Africa" or "Darkness" or "Safari" in your title. Subtitles may include the words "Zanzibar", "Congo", "Big", "Sky", "Shadow", "Drum", "Sun" or "Bygone". After celebrity activists and aid-workers, conservationists are Africa's most important people. Do not offend them.'[2] The essay grew out of a 'long – truly long – rambling email' Wainaina wrote to the magazine's editor in a 'fit of anger, maybe even low blood sugar – it runs in the family'.[3] Frustrated by the narrow bandwidth of tropes that define the African literary landscape, he turned each cliché on its head – and established himself in the process as one of the continent's sharpest and most critical voices.

To most, Wainaina's essay might seem an odd starting place for a discussion about architecture, both in general and across Africa specifically. African projects account for only 12 per cent of all projects submitted for the 13th Award Cycle of the Aga Khan Award for Architecture. Forty-two entries were put forward from East, Central, South and West Africa (North Africa has been excluded from this argument, owing to its obvious cultural relationship with the Islamic world). Africa – as a whole – contributes roughly 30 per cent of the world's Muslim population, which is more than South Asia or the Arabian Peninsula, whose projects make up 9.5 per cent and 14 per cent of the total project list respectively. Yet only four of the submissions were designed or commissioned by African architects and/or clients. The vast majority fall into the aid-development category, generally relying on NGO patronage for design expertise, technical know-how and funding. This is not to say that the projects submitted aren't worthy, *per se;* it's simply that they are remarkably similar in brief, execution and scope. But why does this matter? Should it?

Yes, it does matter – and yes, it should. In some senses, literature and architecture make for strange bedfellows. One: mobile, fleet-of-foot, relatively immediate and cheap to produce; the other: expensive, labour-intensive and time-consuming to make. Yet the two disciplines share a number of fundamentals in common. Churchill's famous maxim, 'we shape our buildings; thereafter they shape us',[4] applies as much to language as it does to architecture: we shape the world through the means by which we describe it, both to ourselves and to others. One might also say architecture is a form of language, if not *the* form of language. As the French philosopher Jacques Derrida argues, 'language can [also] be seen as a prominent architectural concern. Architects approach certain forms, shapes and configurations as the design elements of architecture in the same way they approach word choice, or grammar, or sentence structure.'[5] Infrastructure, dwelling and mythmaking aside, both language and architecture are powerful shapers and vessels of culture – and of cultural identity in particular. This relationship presents a particular dilemma for African architects, most especially for those living and working in Africa. In no specific order, the four official languages of the African Union are Arabic, English, French and Portuguese, none of which are indigenous to the continent's 54 countries. For better or for worse, the colonial encounter between Europe and Africa left more than blood and style in its wake: it fundamentally altered the way Africans express themselves, both in spoken and written language *and* in the built environment. Aside from the obvious linguistic challenges of communicating in a language other than one's mother tongue, at a much deeper level it has permanently compromised, even wounded, the uniquely intimate and intertwined relationship between people and place – the life-force of cultural production in its broadest sense. The implications for African cultural identities are immense. The insistence on 'official' language (a public language, one might call it) at the expense of an indigenous or 'private' (read: domestic) language has brought about its own peculiar pathology, on which every prominent post-colonial or critical theorist from Fanon to Foucault has written. For the most part, contemporary Africans live in an uneasy truce between tradition and modernity, suspended somewhere between aspiration and alienation. It's fair to say that alienation in varying degrees from one's tongue or place *is* the nature of the vast majority of cultural production across Africa at present.

Of course this is not unique to Africa. All artists (in the widest sense of the word) must struggle through what the poet Pablo Neruda calls the 'labyrinths of his/her chosen medium of expression that is an essential condition of being'.[6] As the South African Nobel Laureate Nadine Gordimer writes, 'I doubt if any artist ever finds himself in the ideal condition of Hegel's "individual consciousness in wholly harmonious" relationship to the external power of society'.[7] But there can be few parallels in history where the fundamental balance between people and place has been altered as intensely or violently as it has on the African continent. Sartre sums it up well: 'The exploited experience exploitation *as their reality.*'[8] For the African artist, confronting his or her reality *in order to move beyond it*, is key.

It is against this backdrop that the 42 African projects submitted to this cycle should be read. If 'development' is contemporary Africa's paradigm – Africa's present-day *reality* – the ratio of 4:42, which translates to less than two per cent of all projects undertaken or designed by Africans themselves, *is* the norm: the 'official' architecture of the continent, similar to its 'official' languages, perpetually narrated by outsiders, architecture that is funded and finessed 'on behalf of', seldom 'by'. It is hard – perhaps even impossible – to think of any other context in which such a distorted paradigm might exist. The mere idea of 98 per cent of all American or European projects being done by African or Asian architects is absurd. Yet such is the power of the 'developed/developing' narrative shaping so much of contemporary African architecture that it appears ... well, *normal.* Ninety per cent of the African projects contain the word 'community' or 'development' in their title. There are two restoration projects, no adaptive reuse schemes; no urban masterplans or private residences; a handful of primary schools; no commercial facilities or libraries or museums; and no civic buildings of note. This is emphatically not to say that the projects that have been submitted are in *themselves* wrongfully conceived or executed. There are some extremely well-designed projects on the long list to which one might affix words such as 'iconic', 'meaningful', 'powerful', 'moving', etc. Two such projects are on the shortlist of 19: Japanese–US-based architect Toshiko Mori's Thread Cultural Centre in Senegal and Nigerian architect Kunlé Adeyemi's Makoko Floating School, which has been the subject of much critical acclaim and debate since its construction and subsequent demise. Both projects are remarkable for different reasons: both were photographed by the now-legendary Dutch photographer, Iwan Baan, and both have had their fair share of global renown, and rightly so. Mori designed the structure from New York and did not visit Senegal. Adeyemi, a Lagos resident, built a second prototype, which sailed triumphantly to Venice to collect the Silver Lion. It was infinitely more robust (and useful?) than the original, which sank. Yet, as Angel Borrego Cubero's hilarious yet cutting film, *The Competition*, shows, a site visit is no prerequisite or guarantee of good architecture.

In her provocative anthology, *Playing in the Dark* (1992), the African-American writer Toni Morrison speaks of 'extending the study of American literature into a wider landscape', arguing for the need to 'draw a map of a critical geography and to use that map to open as much space for discovery, intellectual adventure and close exploration as did the original charting of the New World – without the mandate for conquest'.[9] It is a compelling thought: to similarly extend the study, scope and praxis of African architecture into a wider landscape than that of charitable works focused almost exclusively on social gain. A *Time* magazine article dated 4 March 1957, two days before independence in the Gold Coast (now Ghana), is revealing:

> Architect Harry Weese was in trouble. He had just arrived in Accra, the palm-fringed capital of West Africa's Gold Coast and what had seemed like a minor problem back in his Chicago office suddenly began growing like a tropical weed. Young, function-minded architect Weese had been commissioned by the State Department on a low budget of 300,000 USD to design an embassy and staff residences in hot, humid Accra with the stipulation that his design must harmonise with the indigenous architectural tradition. But apart from thatch or corrugated iron and mud, he found that there was no indigenous architecture, let alone any tradition, to harmonise with. About the only buildings that could qualify as architecture were some modern boxy structures put up by Europeans. But they were Mediterranean in style, not equatorial. Telling himself that, 'If there is no native architectural tradition, you have to start one', he set about solving his problem. Stone-and-steel man Weese went native.[10]

In the 1950s and 1960s, as the winds of change swept across Africa and Asia, signalling the end of empire, the modern movement's preoccupation with the social forces surrounding architecture, specifically 'progress' and 'development', dovetailed neatly with the emerging discourses of independence. At the same time, in European and American capitals, an approach that came to be known as 'tropical architecture' was beginning to take root, established as a *bona fide* term through its representation in avant-garde publications and the establishment of an approved curriculum at an elite school (Architectural Association). This architecture was in the International Style – clean, functional and non-site-specific. With its emphasis on health and sanitation and the appeal of belonging to a cosmopolitan world 'club', it was taken up enthusiastically by many of the newly independent African leaders, including Kwame Nkrumah. With hindsight, the ambitions and aspirations seem obvious, even touching. In the decade following independence in Ghana in the 1960s, Nkrumah embarked on what is now seen as the most ambitious building programme in West African history, focusing primarily on educational buildings, which, as the historian Udo Kultermann has noted, 'was no accident. The most significant architectural achievements in Africa are to be found among educational buildings. It ranks before all economic, political and military considerations.'[11]

Nearly 60 years later, that ambition seems to have run its course. There are few, if any, educational buildings that could reasonably be construed as 'significant' outside the paradigm of pressing, sometimes desperate need. Indeed, educational infrastructure can no longer be said to rank before all other considerations. It is in this context that the 'development bind' is most readily apparent. By limiting the vocabulary and language of architecture to a single context, we limit the scope of future African (and outsider) voices. Since its inception, the Aga Khan Award for Architecture has consistently encouraged entrants, jurors and critics alike to demonstrate their trust in pluralism and in the values and benefits of diverse and multiple approaches. The invitation to think across boundaries – whether of culture, class or caste – extends to the way we think about architectural language, programme and form. Africa is not one country, to paraphrase Wainaina. Neither is it one tongue, one voice, one vision or one type. Now, perhaps more than ever, the cultural pluralism that the Award celebrates should be pushed to Africa's fore.

1 Definition taken from *Oxford English Dictionary*. [O]. Accessed 27 July 2016.
2 Binyavanga Wainaina, 'How To Write About Africa', *Granta* 92 (2005).
3 Quoted in Alexis Okeowo's article, 'Binyavanga Wainaina's Africa', *The New Yorker*, 17 August 2010. [O]. http://www.newyorker.com/books/page-turner/binyavanga-wainainas-africa. Accessed 19 July 2016.
4 Winston Churchill (1874–1965), cited in Randal O'Toole *The Best-Laid Plans* (Washington DC: Cato Institute, 2007), 161.
5 Jacques Derrida, 'Architecture: Where The Desire May Live', *Domus* 671 (1986), 25.
6 Pablo Neruda, *Memoirs*, translated by H St Martin (London: Souvenir Press, 1977)
7 Nadine Gordimer, 'Relevance and Commitment', *The Essential Gesture* (London: Penguin, 1988), 135.
8 Jean-Paul Sartre, 'Racism and Colonialism as Praxis and Process', *Critique of Dialectical Reason*, Jean-Paul Sartre Archive 1905–1960. [O]. https://www.marxists.org/reference/archive/sartre/works/critic/racism-algeria.htm. Accessed 18 July 2016.
9 Toni Morrison, *Playing in the Dark: Whiteness and the Literary Imagination* (Cambridge, MA: Harvard University Press, 1992), 3.
10 Taken from *Time* magazine, 4 March 1957. [O]. www.time.com/time/magazine/article/0,9171,862485,00.html. Retrieved 6 June 2007.
11 Udo Kultermann, *New Directions in African Architecture* (New York: George Braziller, 1969).

Manouchehri House

Kashan, Iran

Kashan is a historic city in the Iranian province of Isfahan. The setting for Shah Abbas I's famous garden, Bagh-e Fin, it was also renowned for its crafts traditions, including glazed pottery, copperware and textiles – Kashani brocades of silks and velvets were prized in imperial courts throughout Europe and Asia. Bagh-e Fin and all the other works of Abbas I were razed in a devastating earthquake in 1778, which killed half of the city's inhabitants. But when the time came to rebuild, the merchants made their houses even grander than before, with sophisticated brick masonry and exquisite ornamentation. Mostly closed from the outside, the structures were organised around an internal courtyard, offering a high degree of privacy as well as protection from the desert climate.

These Qajari merchants' houses, many of them long-neglected, are increasingly being renovated by private individuals with an interest in preserving the city's cultural heritage and fading crafts traditions. The Manouchehri House is one such project, an exemplary restoration and adaptive reuse of a nineteenth-century merchant's home. Besides drawing attention to Kashan's architectural heritage, the renovated building raises awareness of its crafts traditions, incorporating a weaving workshop as well as a shop to sell the products of the looms. The house also serves as a small hotel.

The renovation was undertaken by an expert architect and masons with extensive knowledge of local materials and traditional construction techniques. Renderings and finishes include: exterior walls –brickwork and stucco, or mud and hay cob; interior walls and ceilings – mud and stucco (or sometimes fine straw cob); floors in rooms – industrial clay tiles; corridors – brick and cobblestone paving; courtyard and balcony floors – mudbrick tiles; courtyard stairs – Iranian saffron travertine; doors and window frames – maple wood. Mirrorwork was added as decoration in some locations.

And the revitalisation has extended beyond the bounds of the building itself, to take in the immediate surroundings. With its two entrances on the south and north sides, Manouchehri House transforms a formerly austere alleyway into a space for living and sharing.

Client
Saba Manouchehri Kashani, Kashan, Iran

Conservation Team
Abolfazl Ebrahim Shahi, project manager (2007–2014), Kashan, Iran
Seyyed Akbar Helli, traditional architect (2009–2011), Kashan, Iran
Shahnaz Nader Esfahani, interior designer, Tehran, Iran

Restoration Consultants
Farhad Fakhar Tehrani (2009–2011), Mohammad Reza Haeri (2008), Hamidreza Ziarati (2008–2011), Ali Adhami, Kashan, Iran

Electrical Engineer
Ahmad Seyyedi, Kashan, Iran

Mechanical Engineer
Mohsen Moghaddam, Kashan, Iran

Contractors
Seyyed Akbar Helli, general contractor, Kashan, Iran
Mohsen Akbarzadeh, electrical contractor, Kashan, Iran
Mohsen Fellezi, mechanical contractor, Kashan, Iran
Mohsen Shahi, junior contractor, Kashan, Iran

Site Managers
Akbar Arezegar, site manager, Kashan, Iran
Ali Adhami, surveyor, Kashan, Iran

Excavation
Habibollah Ahmadi, excavation, Kashan, Iran

Reinforcement
Reza Arezooie, Kashan, Iran

Vault Cconstruction
Abbas Golkar, Kashan, Iran

Brickworks
Hassan Shamsaie, Ali Rahimi, Reza Bidgoli, Ali Zahedi, Ali Jafari, Kashan, Iran

Carpenter
Hossein Shafaie, Kashan, Iran

Stucco works
Abbas Salmani, Maryam Shakiba, Mohammad Shagerdi, Kashan, Iran

Stonework
Mohammad Mirzapour, Kashan, Iran

Tilework
Mohammadali Shabani, Kashan, Iran

Copperwork
Mohammad Aghajanzadeh, Kashan, Iran

Decorative Limework
Morteza Bolbolmoghadam, Kashan, Iran

Restoration and Revitalisation
Abolfazl Shahi, manager, advisor and graphic artist, Kashan, Iran

Revitalisation Team
Zainab Esmati, hotel manager, Kashan, Iran
Ali Roshan, hotel training manager, Kashan, Iran
Marjan Koochak, textile designer, Kashan, Iran
Ghoramreza Hassanijhe (Mirza), Khalil Ya Allah, Ahmad Tale, Mashaallah Enayati, master weavers, Kashan, Iran
Seyed Reza Ya Allah, Hassan Tale, weavers, Kashan, Iran
Sajjad Tale, Mohsen Niazi, weaving apprentices, Kashan, Iran

Project Data
Site area: 1,370 m^2
Total floor area: 1,495 m^2
Total cost: 1,056,000 USD
Commission: February 2008
Design: March 2008–February 2011
Construction: March 2008–February 2011
Completion: March 2011

Saba Manouchehri is an Iranian multidisciplinary artist. She studied jewellery and metalsmithing at the School of the Museum of Fine Arts in Boston and received her fine arts degree from Tufts University. Her interest in finding value in the neglected and forgotten manifests itself in her works as well as her large-scale urban renewal projects. Recycling and upcycling have been at the heart of her creations. In her jewellery and sculptures, from the abandoned to the ignored, she brings back life to broken and discarded objects by giving them a new assemblage and therefore new spirit and meaning. She collects Iranian art and textiles and is working intensely towards the revival of traditional weaving arts in Kashan.

In 2008, inspired to revive the potential beauty of a neglected and near-ruined traditional house and neighbourhood, the restoration and revitalisation of Manouchehri House became her passion, ably assisted in this task by an expert group of restoration consultants and conservation managers.

Manouchehri has received the JOSTAR Prize, the first national prize for quality in urban renewal participation from the Ministry of Housing and Urban Development. In 2015 she also received the National Heritage Award for Reviving the Art of Brocade from the Iran Cultural Heritage, Handicrafts and Tourism Organization.

Abolfazl Ebrahim Shahi is an Iranian artist. After obtaining his undergraduate degree in graphic design, he completed a master's degree in theology from the Islamic Azad University of Tehran. His work in reviving traditional Persian arts and crafts has been inspired by the aesthetics of the Saqqakhaneh school of art.

Seyyed Akbar Helli is an Iranian self-taught traditional architect. He started working as a mason from the age of 13 and learnt from notable Kashani traditional architects before becoming an independent master himself. Helli has worked on numerous restoration projects with the Kashan Municipality and Isfahan Cultural Heritage, Handicrafts and Tourism Organisation, and taught architecture at the Kashan University of Art and Architecture from 1996–2008.

Shahnaz Nader is an Iranian interior designer. She holds an interior design degree from the New York School of Interior Design and has worked on various interior design projects since the 1970s. She has dedicated herself to making handicrafts and furniture using Iranian traditional techniques while modifying those designs and patterns in unique and innovative ways.

Website
www.manouchehrihouse.com

0
50
100
150

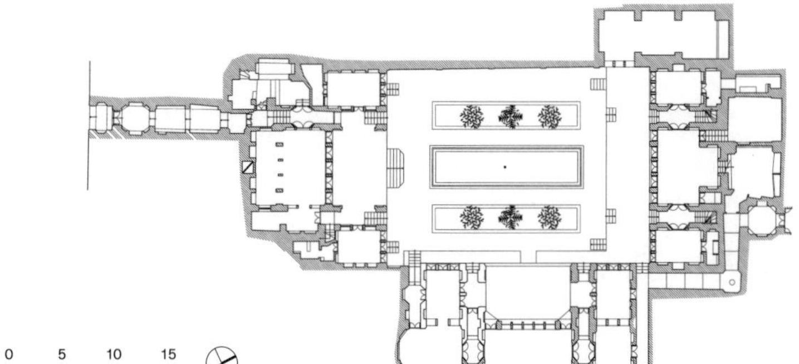
0
5
10
15

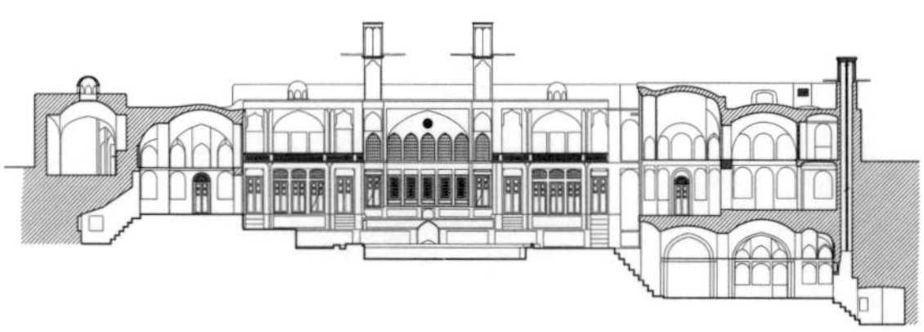

Nasrid Tower Restoration

Huercal-Overa, Spain

The Nasrid Tower has stood for centuries on a forbidding hilltop in eastern Andalusia. Visible from a great distance, its defensive function is immediately clear: 700 years ago, this was a marker of the Muslim frontier, a beacon warning local inhabitants of approaching raids. In restoring the structure and making it accessible, the architects have sought to contrast the tower's sense of permanence with the ephemerality of their own interventions – an approach that recalls the 'intentional flaws' of Islamic art. In their words: 'The project explores the dichotomy between the solid, ageless construction of the existing Nasrid Tower, made by anonymous craftsmen, and the provisional, light, degradable nature of the contemporary. The additions to the original building are conceived as future ruins: removable, temporary objects with a short lifespan, which will deteriorate and eventually be replaced.'

While the restoration of the tower itself meticulously replaces like for like (lime mortar and rammed earth), the interventions are visibly modern. Two structures made of weathering steel provide the necessary new facilities. One, resembling a shipping container, holds an office and visitor toilets. The other, shaped like a barrel or drum, wraps around the spiral staircase that reinstates the original access point to the tower. The drum is semi-open, and the platform at the top recalls the tower's primary role as a lookout. But where the old tower is rectilinear and massive, the new stair tower is cylindrical and hollow; where the old structure is light and eye-catching, the new one is dark and sober. The complementarity of geometry, form and material has been carefully considered throughout.

An imposing flight of steps leading up to the tower (a legacy of the previous owner) was replaced with an approach more in harmony with the landscape – a meandering path dotted with seating areas for visitors to enjoy the views. Concrete and mortar was used for both the exterior paving and the benches, while the discreet fencing is made of pre-rusted steel, in keeping with many of the other interventions.

Client
Municipality of Huercal-Overa, Spain:
Domingo Fernandez Zurano, mayor
Jose María Soler Carmona, deputy head
Elena Sánchez Castellón, historian, site cultural management

Junta de Andalucía, Department of Cultural Affairs, Almería, Spain:
Rosa Aguilar Rivero, minister of culture
Alfredo Valdivia Ayala, representative of the department of culture
Juan Dominguez Carreño, head of the restoration department

Architects
Castillo Miras Arquitectos, Madrid/Almería, Spain:
Luis Castillo Villegas, Mercedes Miras Varela, partners

Contractor
Construcciones José Lorenzo, Almeria, Spain:
José Luis Lorenzo Jimenez, construction and conservation manager

Site Supervisor
Luis Hervas López, Almería, Spain

Structural Engineer
Satec Ingenieros, Almería, Spain:
Manuel López Romero

Project Data
Site area: 3,500 m^2
Ground floor area: 223 m^2
Cost: 790,000 USD
Commission: January 2005
Design: November 2005–February 2006
Construction: January 2009–December 2009
Occupancy: March 2010

Castillo Miras Arquitectos
Castillo Miras Arquitectos is an architectural office based in Almería, a coastal town in the Spanish region of Andalusia. Mercedes Miras studied architecture at Escuela Técnica Superior de Arquitectura de Sevilla (ETSAS), completing her diploma in 1997. Her work has been concerned mainly with restoration and preservation of historical buildings, including the renovation to house the Andalusian Photography Museum. Luis Castillo studied architecture at the Escuela Técnica Superior de Arquitectura de Madrid (ETSAM) and the Architectural Association (AA), completing his diploma in 1995 and afterwards working in several practices in Spain and The Netherlands.

Their practice deals with concepts such as recycling, reusing the obsolete and reclaiming degraded structures, spaces and landscapes. They are part of a new architectural sensibility that take these strategies as a starting point, rejecting the 'artistification' of architecture as well as its transmutation into a commodity for mass consumption.

Their work and essays have been featured in prestigious publications such as *Casabella, Arquitectura Viva, Detail* and *OASE.*

Website
www.castillomiras.es

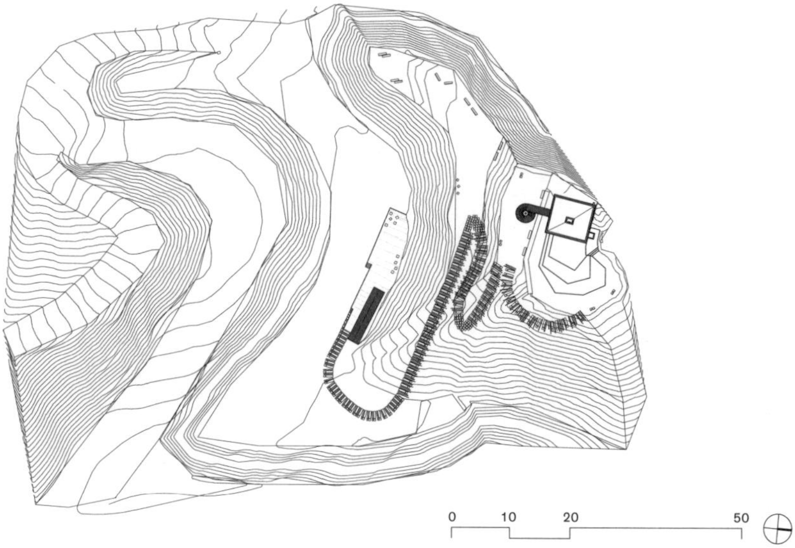
0
10
20
50

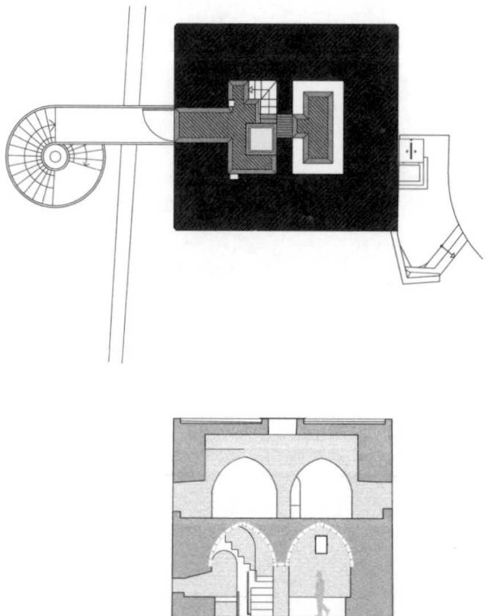

A Sensitive Boldness in Conservation

Seif El Rashidi

Among the aims of the Aga Khan Award for Architecture is to recognise outstanding projects which enhance the built environment in places with links to Islamic civilisation, past or present. In doing so, it draws attention to exemplary approaches to architecture, inspiring others further afield. The restoration of a Nasrid Tower near Almería in Andalusia, and the construction of a new library over the archaeological remains of a medieval Muslim settlement in Ceuta, a Spanish enclave in North Africa, both finalists in this cycle, present masterful solutions to a series of difficult conservation and design challenges faced by architects and local governments the world over.

In the case of the project in Andalusia, a key challenge was what to do with a derelict medieval building for which there was no obvious use – a tower with very limited floor space on a rocky outcrop at some distance from the small town of Huercal-Overa. The architects' response was both pragmatic and imaginative, seeking to reinstate the romantic allure of the dramatic yet simple building and to restore its rugged landscape evoking the trials and tribulations of the Arabs in fourteenth-century Spain. The tower's dual role as a lookout and a beacon (to warn neighbouring townspeople of imminent threat) was a driving idea behind the work of Mercedes Miras and Luis Castillo. Their intervention has enabled the building to become an important feature of Huercal-Overa's identity and a venue for community events without destroying the sense of adventure attained on finally reaching the imposing edifice perched on its hilltop.

In more practical terms, the architectural intervention required thinking critically about which of the later changes to the medieval tower to strip away, and which to retain as a record of its long history. The architects' approach was to keep any modifications that continued to use and celebrate the tower's original defensive function – namely, gun slits and hideouts added during a more recent divisive conflict, the Spanish Civil War – but to remove the assortment of later decorative elements added by a local grandee, which were out of keeping with the building's original function and its economy of line and material.

Most remarkable, from the design point of view, is the balance attained between the preservation of the historic fabric and the modern interventions enabling public access and use. Castillo and Miras' philosophy was that, in the grand scheme of things, their intervention would be a fleeting episode in the long and venerable history of the medieval building. As such, they conceived their additions to just lightly touch both the landscape and the original structure, to contrast in form, material, colour, to pay homage to the bold geometry of the tower and, perhaps most poignantly, by choosing a finish of prerusted steel, to embody the idea of their modern intervention as being ephemeral – and already in the process of decay. Their key physical interventions – a barrel-like staircase tower, and a container housing offices and toilet facilities – are described by the couple as being like objets trouvés – things that serve a purpose for a brief period and then are cast aside.

Some may ask: 'So what, how is this different from any other scheme?' The answer, really, is in the quality and thoughtfulness of their work: in the way, for example, the patina and pockmarks of history have been preserved even while the original lime mortar has been cleaned to give the tower a moonlit sheen; or in the way the restored sections are distinct, but neither garish nor harsh, while the concrete paths and seating cubes are the perfect shade of honeyish grey. 'How?', one must ask. 'Many, many site trials', Castillo and Miras respond.

As an architectural statement there is another mastery – that the strong form of their own tower is the perfect complement to the Nasrid building; that it is impressive, but from a distance, subservient, and that it too is a lookout, an *atalaya.*

Facebook gives an indication of the tower's popularity, even as a setting for weddings, where silky chairs and gauzy blue ribbons are in order. What? Yes, indeed. Though many of the users may find it hard to pinpoint what it is that makes the scheme work, they know that they like it – and the local council has found a tour guide/animator to give the place another kind of soul, telling its story, mainly to locals.

Can it serve as a model? Certainly. Anyone could, in theory, achieve what Castillo and Miras have done here. But it would take diligence, dedication, the honing of skills, confidence, and yet great subtlety to attain the right balance. This project, then, is also a beacon, a lighthouse, of what can *occasionally* be achieved.

The second project, Ceuta Public Library, exists in the most curious of places – a multicultural (Moroccan-Spanish) border region of Spain, actually in mainland North Africa. Excavations on a site earmarked for mixed-use development revealed unexpectedly important archaeological remains of a wealthy Muslim community that had fled the Spanish mainland in the fourteenth century. The archaeologist's persistence, coupled with the visionary support of municipal representatives, enabled a change in direction: the decision to use the site for cultural purposes, in order to preserve the archaeology, making a feature out of it. This achievement merits a pause for reflection: in most places of the world, archaeological value pales against urban development's financial lure.

A public competition attracted national interest, with the winning scheme chosen because it was energised by the very challenges posed by the site. The library constructed over the ruins by Angela de Paredes and Ignacio Pedrosa does more, though, than integrate the now-preserved remains of a Muslim city into a slick modern building. It overcomes a challenging topography, creating a sculptural, clean-lined edifice whose texture and magnificent form hint at the city's medieval defences – a refreshing response in a place where there are no apparent links between architecture past and present, and where, overall, the building stock is pretty ordinary. The interior is light, legible, logical; a space conducive to labour and leisure alike. To counteract the blinding glare of the Mediterranean sun, Pedrosa and de Paredes resort to an age-old solution engrained in the architectural DNA of the Islamic world: screening. And their design is perfectly practical and utilitarian – straightforward prefabricated perforated sheets, accessible to clean and easily replaceable. These last details speak of an architectural practice as committed to the building's function as to its aesthetic quality. Pedrosa and de Paredes know full well the challenges of maintaining public buildings beyond the availability of an initial pot of funding: they build for robustness, for the future. 'Remember that we have no current government', they say.

The outcome is best conveyed by the spirit of the public library, a well-used social space where the residents of Ceuta want to come, not just because of its resources but, critically, because it is an environment where they feel comfortable and creative; where they can delve in solitude into their own personal quests – a new CV, a law exam – or work as a group, or think and daydream as they peer beyond the uplifting white book-filled spaces through the screens to horizons blue.

Where this library really wins is in answer to the questions of how and whom it serves – which is everyone, from head-scarved youths reading Spanish literature, to researchers in need of a microfilm collection, conference-going archaeologists, local art groups, musical prodigies and older residents of the city-region delighted with a space where they can experience the creative energy of Ceuta's youth. It speaks of multifaceted identities and comfortable diversity. 'It has brought life to the area', a neighbour says. Scurrying to move furniture to turn the entrance space by the archaeological site into a venue for an evening recital, the director and his team are beaming. (The number of pages in their logbook of cultural events already far exceeds the number of days.) The project archaeologist and the municipal director of cultural affairs, not to mention the two architects, stand proud.

In some respects the library, as both a great building and a community space, has eclipsed the archaeological site at its core. Some would argue that, fairly or unfairly, this may have cost it an Aga Khan Award, just as the Nasrid Tower project's seeming effortlessness may have diminished the sense of what it achieves.

Commiserations aside, both of these projects have great lessons to share. To a world stumped by the challenges of hard-to-use built heritage, they show just what can effectively be achieved. 'Building around the archaeological site was technically easy', Ignacio Pedrosa shrugs, when asked. There is an answer here powerful enough to keep at bay the illicit bulldozers and the archaeological cordons. And on the forbidding hilltop in Huercal-Overa is a confirmation of how everyday, normal communities can connect with their heritage: allow them to use it, to enjoy it, and allow yourselves to be inspired. The message of these two government-sponsored projects in a resource- and idea-strapped age is clear: *learn!*

House of 40 Knots

Tehran, Iran

The House of 40 Knots stands out amid the rather monotonous block structure of west Tehran. Departing from the rectilinear order of the neighbouring residential buildings, its layered facade joins elements of two Iranian traditions – carpet-weaving and brick – in a creative reinterpretation of the mashrabiyya. The traditional Persian method of weaving consists of two people working together, one reciting instructions while the other sits at the loom, making the corresponding knots in the carpet. The handmade exterior of this residence, built by labourers who were unable to read technical drawings, was produced using a similar system. As the supervising mason called out instructions, a team of seven workers placed the bricks, one by one, on reinforcement bars, creating an irregular, projecting surface that is partly structural rather than just a veneer. Trained in situ, the formerly unskilled labourers became proficient in performing specialised work.

The patterns of the woven facade relate to the path of the sun. They allow for natural ventilation and dampen noise. Crucially, where windows sit behind the brick screen, the filtered natural light forms a textured grid that illuminates the internal spaces while maintaining the residents' privacy. A concern with privacy also shaped the arrangement of the interior. In each of the ten apartments a glass door creates a buffer space between the public staircase and the domestic realm: when the door of the apartment is open, there are no direct views inside. In addition, the plan makes a clear distinction between private space – two bedrooms and a bathroom used only by the household – and the area accessible to both residents and guests, consisting of a living room, kitchen/dining room and a second bathroom.

Common areas and parking are located on the ground floor and basement, while there are two apartments on each of the five upper storeys. Designed for middle-income families, the units range in size from 75 m^2 to 88 m^2. The main structure is a steel frame erected on concrete foundations. Inspired by local technologies and utilising local materials and labour, this is a contemporary residential building that responds to local social and environmental contexts.

پارکینگ واحد
7 / ٧

Client
Alireza Zahed, Tehran, Iran

Architects
Habibeh Madjdabadi, Alireza Mashhadimirza, Tehran, Iran
Mani Shabanzadeh, Hamid Zinsaz, Parastoo Noroozi, design team, Tehran, Iran

Architect of Record
Alireza Mashhadimirza, Tehran, Iran

Structural Engineer
Esameel Tabatabayi, Tehran, Iran

Mechanical Engineer
Hossein Monfared, Tehran, Iran

Brickworks
Soheil Company, Tehran, Iran

Brickwork Contractor
RTA Company, Tehran, Iran

Project Data
Site area: 245 m^2
Total floor area: 1,370 m^2
Cost: 430,000 USD
Commission: February 2012
Design: May 2012–December 2012
Construction: October 2012–August 2013
Occupancy: April 2014

Habibeh Madjdabadi
Habibeh Madjdabadi established her design office in 2000 after winning first prize in a design competition for restoring historic buildings in Iran. She has recently worked on the design of the Norwegian Embassy in Tehran, combining brick and mirror on the facade, in collaboration with Intertecno of Italy. Materials are an important means of expression in Madjdabadi's work and she considers them from a poetic point of view. In recent years, she has shown a particular interest in the mirror as a traditional and contemporary material. Her installation entitled *Death of the Author* is a space created by hundreds of mirror fragments and Persian alphabet letters arranged inside an old room belonging to an Art Deco house of the 1930s.

Madjdabadi has published widely in Iranian architecture magazines and she is a member of the editorial board of *Me'mar* magazine.

Alireza Mashhadimirza
Alireza Mashhadimirza is an Iranian practising architect, university-level educator and researcher on architecture. He was born and grew up in Tehran within a cultured family, graduating with a master's degree from the school of architecture at Elm o Sanat University (Iran University of Science & Technology) in 1999 and establishing his own architectural office thereafter. His design work ranges from interiors and architecture to urban spaces and landscape and he has won national and international design awards. Mashhadimirza has received national recognition for his training and workshop tours at architecture schools all over the nation, designed to engender a creativity beyond the ordinary and to introduce his philosophy under the titles of *The Sounds of Architecture* and *The Lyrics of Brick Installation*. He is currently lecturer at the school of architecture at Azad Islamic University. His research and publications, in both Persian and English, are recognised as valuable contributions towards architectural education in Iran.

Habibeh Madjdabadi and Alireza Mashhadimirza have collaborated on a number of projects and competitions. The House of 40 Knots was shortlisted at the 2014 Worldwide Brick Award and gained third place in the 2014 Me'mar awards, and they received a Chicago Athenaeum Award in 2014 for Mellat Bank's copper facade.

Websites
www.habibehmadjdabadi.com
www.mashhadimirza.com

0
1
2

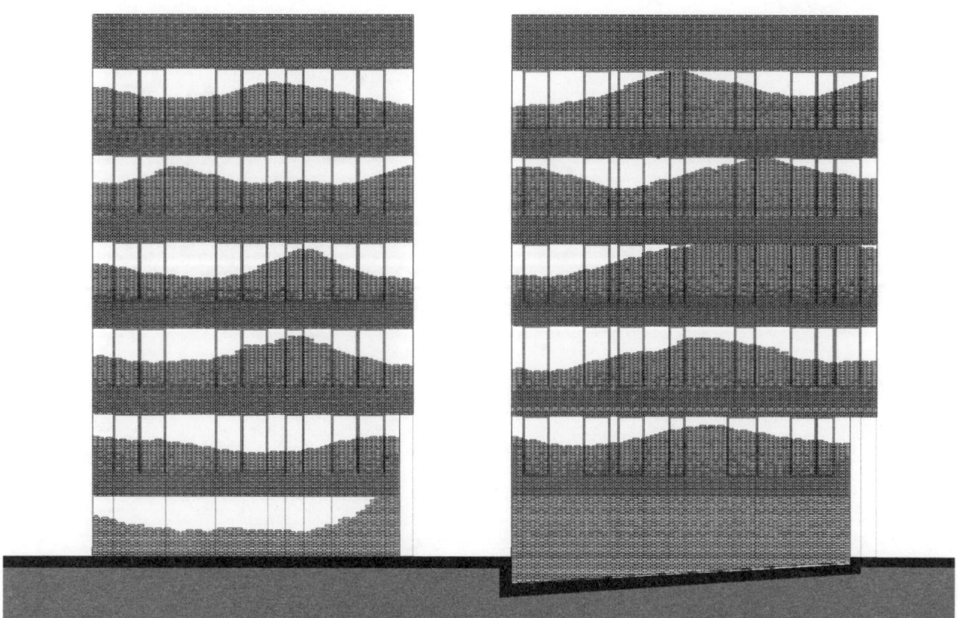

Casa-Port New Railway Station

Casablanca, Morocco

In the heart of Casablanca, connecting the Medina and Art Deco districts to the fast-growing port area, the city's new railway station integrates vernacular architectural traditions into an avowedly modernist structure. More than just a piece of transport infrastructure, Casa-Port is both a symbol of the city's heritage and a statement of confidence in its future.

Unlike the previous station on the site, which simply terminated Boulevard Houphouët Boigny, Casa-Port is oriented in a way that allows for traffic flows to the developing parts of the city. Besides handling rising numbers of rail passengers – a projected 25 million a year – it serves as an interchange hub for the city's other transport systems (buses and trams). A wide entrance plaza leads to the main hall, centred around an atrium that opens onto the lower levels of the station. The first basement level contains retail space, including a food court; the levels below are for parking. Concrete is used extensively on the underground levels, while the main circulation spaces are covered in slabs of Slimane limestone, quarried some 80 km away.

The steel canopy roof extends beyond the facades to provide shading. The canopy is supported by slender columns made of concrete (at the lower levels) and steel (from the ground floor up). At the top, the columns split into eight branches to frame sky openings that increase the levels of natural light in the interior, making it easier to navigate through. The ceiling is clad in timber – an evocation of Moroccan architectural traditions. The most sophisticated updating of tradition, however, is to be found on the southwest facade, in the fibre-reinforced concrete mashrabiyya system that provides protection from the glare of the afternoon sun.

The project is a collaboration between AREP, a French company with extensive knowledge in the design of railway stations, and G3A Architects from Morocco. The outcome is a technically sophisticated building that accommodates the complex functional needs of the station infrastructure while also contributing to the cultural and social life of the city of Casablanca – a true urban marker.

BMCE BANK
DIAMANTIN

Client
Office National des Chemins de Fer (ONCF), Rabat, Morocco:
Mohammed Smouni, director of development unit
Mohammed Chahid, director of heritage development

Architects
AREP, Paris, France:
Etienne Tricaud, principal
Philippe Druesne, Christophe Iliou, project team

Groupe 3 Architectes, Rabat, Morocco:
Skander Amine, Omar Tijani, associate architects
Vincent Missemer, project manager

Consultants
MaP3, Paris France:
Emmanuel Livadiotti, founder
Érick Cuervo, structural engineer

UTECA/INGECOBAT, Rabat, Morocco, structural and technical consultants

Atelier Bertrand HOUIN, Rabat, Morocco, landscape architect

Project Data
Total site area: 38,000 m^2
Built area: 33,500 m^2
Cost: 41,000,000 USD
Commission: January 2007
Design: January 2007–November 2010
Construction: May 2008–September 2014
Completion: September 2014

AREP
Since its creation in 1997 by Jean-Marie Duthilleul and Etienne Tricaud – both architects and engineers – AREP has been designing and building for the contemporary city, the nerve centre of mobility. AREP brings together 750 people and some 30 nationalities, involved in more than 800 projects both in France and abroad. Their teams combine various complementary disciplines in a spirit of innovation and attention to human needs: architects, city planners, designers, engineers, economists, architectural programming consultants and construction operations managers.

Having developed a creative approach to public space, which takes into consideration the needs of city dwellers, AREP is a laboratory for ongoing research into the fast-changing urban environment at every scale, from entire metropolitan areas to individual buildings.
AREP is a wholly owned subsidiary of SNCF.

Groupe 3 Architectes (G3A)
Founded in Rabat in 2000 by Skander Amine and Omar Tijani, Groupe 3 Architectes gathers a team of 35 collaborators, including 15 architects. The firm has a multidisciplinary and a culturally diverse team whose professional expertise is constantly fostered by a clear collective intelligence serving its architectural projects. Driven by a permanent search for quality, the firm's partners along with their collaborators embrace values representing the basis of the firm's overall projects: to listen, and to be rigorous and innovative. The firm stands out nationally with its projects in various sectors, providing unique architectural solutions while always aware of geographical and cultural context.

Groupe 3 Architectes is gaining increasing visibility and recognition internationally. In 2013 the firm won the competition for an international office building in Dakar and was on the shortlist competing to design the new Olympic headquarters in Lausanne, while the Mohammed VI Football Academy has been nominated for an Aga Khan Award. In 2014, Groupe 3 Architectes participated in the Venice Architecture Biennale.

Website
www.arep.fr
www.groupe3architectes.com

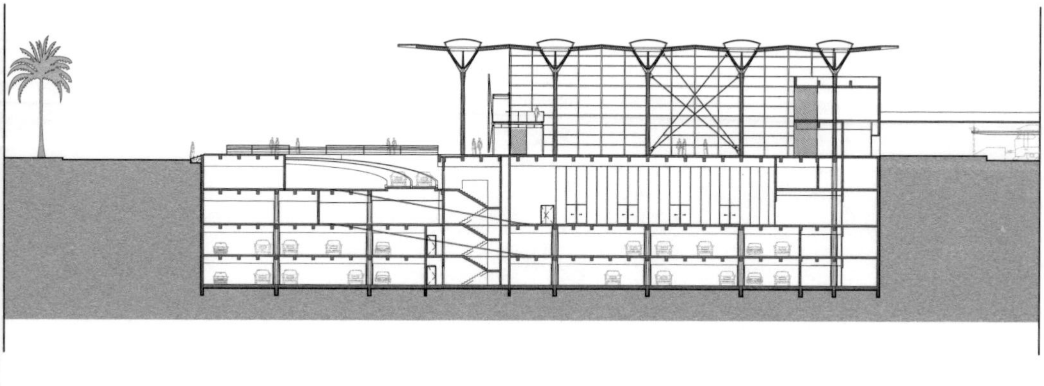
0
5
10
15

Tickets
Abonnement
Police
Accès Voies
Sanitaires
Salle de Prière

Makoko Floating School

Lagos, Nigeria

The Floating School is a small 'watercraft' that expands the facilities of the only school in Makoko, an informal settlement on the edges of the mainland of Lagos. Like many other water communities, Makoko faces challenges of land tenure, lack of public services and inadequate response to flooding and climate change. Conceived as a replicable prototype, the Floating School offers an innovative response to these challenges, being simultaneously an educational facility and a space for community use.

The school is an A-shaped frame with exposed structure – a robust skeleton of wood and bamboo poles. There is no real ornamentation, apart from the elegance of its structural articulation and assembly. Though almost symmetrical along its longitudinal axis, the structure's exterior treatment clearly identifies a weather side (towards the lagoon) and a lee side (towards the mainland), so continuing the analogy with a sailboat. The weather side is more closed, largely covered by roof sheeting, whereas the lee side houses service spaces and the staircase that links the three levels – an open 100 m^2 space on the first level, a 50 m^2 enclosed classroom on the second level, and a 50 m^2 semi-enclosed multipurpose terrace on top. The 2.5 m × 2.5 m modularity of the square plan is repeated in the elevation, and the triangular profile of the whole is carried through the lateral bracings. The experimental approach of merging a fairly standard A-frame structure with a floating raft was conceived to allow local carpenters to manage the construction process.

The project is not a conventional response to a brief, but a statement of at least two intentions. Besides providing much-needed additional school space for the community's children, it was designed to put Makoko on the map and to marshall resistance to the Nigerian government's plan to evict the inhabitants of the settlement. Conceptually, the 'watercraft' structure is intended to be self-sustaining and adaptable to a variety of building typologies, so gradually cultivating an improved quality of architecture, urbanism and living on water.

Clients
Makoko Waterfront Community, Lagos, Nigeria:
Emmanuel Shemede, Noah Jesutin Shemede,
Jeunbete Shemede, Baales of Makoko/Iwaya Waterfront Community

Makoko Community Development Association & Youth Leaders, Lagos, Nigeria

Makoko Floating School Building Team, Lagos, Nigeria

Architect
NLÉ, Amsterdam, The Netherlands:
Kunlé Adeyemi, principal
Lisa Anderson, Thijs Bouman, Leslie Ebony, Marije Nederveen, Segun Omodele, Adekunle Olusola, Chryso Onisiforou, Martin Oreoluwa, Berend Strijland, Monica Velasco, project team

Technical Collaborators
BKVV Architects, Amsterdam, The Netherlands
Dykstra – Naval Architects, Amsterdam, The Netherlands
Pieters Bouwtechniek, structural engineer, The Netherlands
Thieu Besselink, Amsterdam, The Netherlands
SPCIT, Amsterdam, The Netherlands
Roel Bosch Architecten, Rotterdam, The Netherlands
Ikeyi & Arifayan, advisor, Lagos, Nigeria
Matrix Design & Works Nig Ltd, Lagos, Nigeria
Solarmate Engineering Ltd, Lagos, Nigeria

Project Data
Total built area: 220 m^2
Cost: 50,900 USD
Commission: May 2011
Design: December 2011–November 2012
Construction: September 2012–May 2013
Completion: 2013

NLÉ
Founded in 2010, NLÉ, which means 'at home' in Yoruba, is an architecture, design and urbanism practice focused on developing cities and communities. It is led by Kunlé Adeyemi, an architect, designer and urbanist with a track record of conceiving and completing high-profile, high-quality projects internationally.

Born and raised in Nigeria, Adeyemi studied architecture at the University of Lagos where he began his early practice before joining the world-renowned Office for Metropolitan Architecture (OMA) in 2002. At OMA, working closely with founder Rem Koolhaas for nearly a decade, he led the design, development and execution of numerous projects in Europe, Asia, Africa and the Middle East. Among these projects were the award-winning Samsung Museum of Art, Seoul National University Museum, NM Rothschild Bank in London, Shenzhen Stock Exchange tower in China, Prada Transformer in South Korea, Qatar National Library, Qatar Foundation Headquarters and the 4th Mainland Bridge and Masterplan in Lagos. Adeyemi was responsible for critical stages in the design and realisation of these projects. This involved leading OMA's design team, coordinating a global network of stakeholders and expert collaborators, including Arup for engineering and Davis Langdon (AECOM) on cost matters.

Website
www.nleworks.com

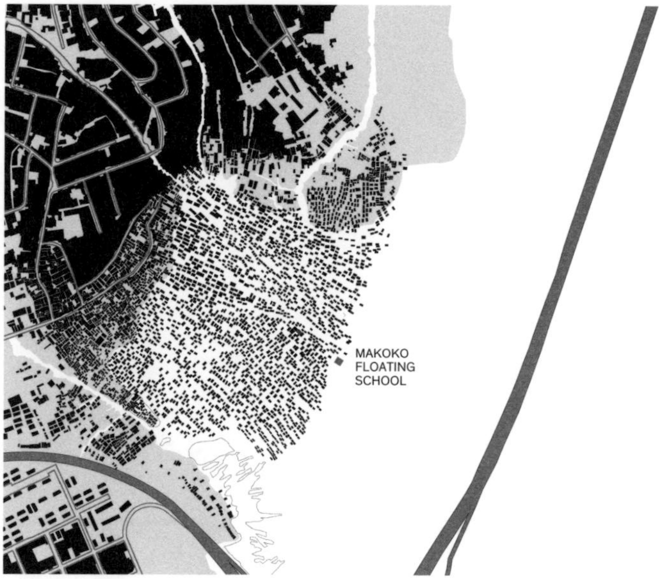
MAKOKO
FLOATING
SCHOOL

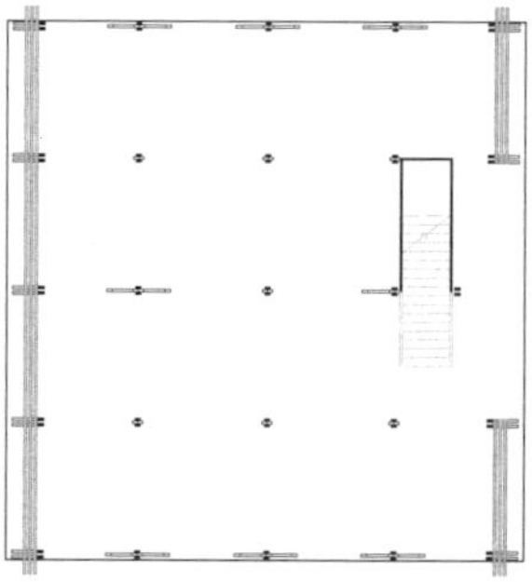

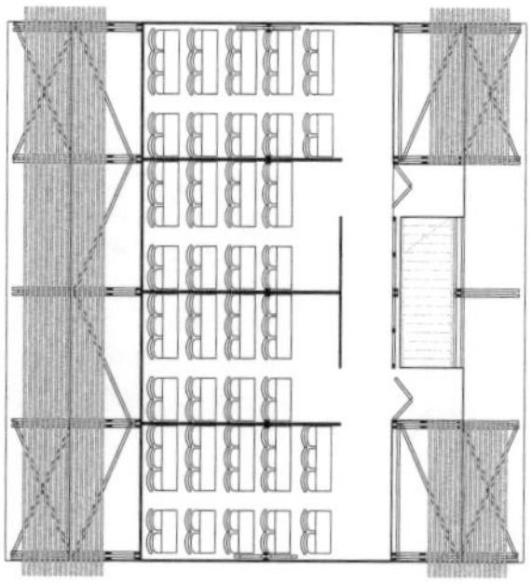

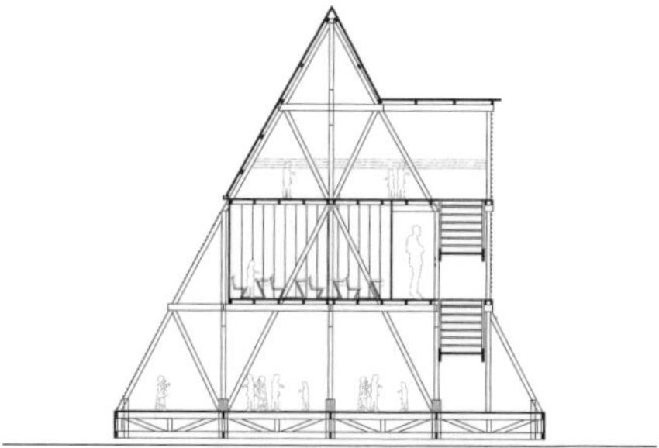

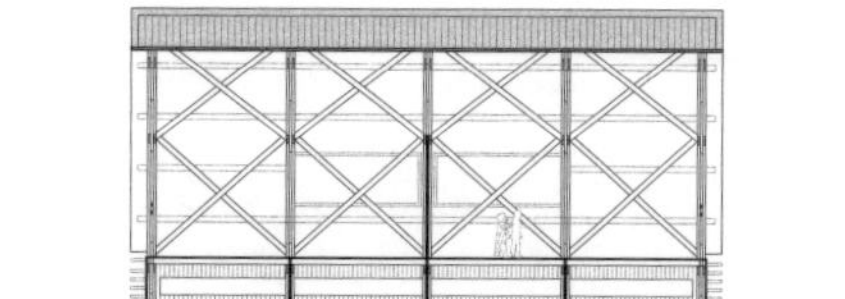

0 1 2 5

Makoko Floating School, Lagos, Nigeria

Ecosystemic Agencies

Tomà Berlanda

Narratives

Dr Magueye Ba is a Senegalese doctor who, after completing his medical studies in Dakar, made a commitment to live in Sinthian, a remote village in the eastern Senegal region of Tambacounda, where he had previously interned as a student. Here he has lived for the last 15 years, dedicating himself to improving the local population's access to medical services. During this time his connection with a growing network of donors, and in particular the partnership with Nicholas Fox Weber of the Josef and Anni Albers Foundation, has been instrumental in securing funding to support modern medical practices in this rural area. Specifically, it has allowed the establishment of the Sinthian Health Centre (the only one with an in-house doctor within a range of 60 km), the construction and running of a pre-school and, most recently, the creation of the Thread Cultural Centre, designed by Toshiko Mori Architect.

Noah Shemede is the founder and principal of the Whanyinna nursery and primary school in Makoko, Lagos, Nigeria. He is also the youngest brother of *Baale* Emmanuel Shemede, one of the leaders of the Iwaya/Makoko waterfront community. Like the majority of the Egun population living in Makoko, the Shemede family has been there for over 100 years and, like many others, they rely on fishing as their main source of income. Noah, the youngest of 22 children, was the only one in his family to receive formal education, an experience that spurred his own interest in pedagogy and empowering children from a very early age. He established the school in 2008, using money set aside from the proceeds of his fishing business. In 2011 he befriended the architect Kunlé Adeyemi and facilitated his connection with the community, a move that later led to the construction of the Makoko Floating School. International awareness of the project has enabled him to access donations to support and expand the operations of the Whanyinna school.

Dr Ba and Noah are central figures in two of the shortlisted projects in this cycle of the Aga Khan Award for Architecture. Meeting with them, in my capacity as technical reviewer, was a privileged occasion to garner insights on the ecosystems that underpin the effectiveness of architecture. In my view, the physical presence of building materials and their logical tectonics should not overshadow an understanding of the extremely prominent position that both these buildings – incidentally the only two projects from sub-Saharan Africa shortlisted this time round – occupy within their physical and human context.

Building on my experience, the reflections that follow are an attempt at capturing three issues raised by the work. One is the relationship between space and society. The second is the relationship between design and community. The third considers the agency of capital.

Environments

One way to convey the challenge of operating within underprivileged and marginalised communities is to locate the architectural act in relation to processes of social and political emancipation. Given that it is essentially the preserve of the privileged few who have access to it and know how to use it, the discipline is susceptible to favouring the interests of architects themselves. Already in 1975, in a paper prepared for the 'Housing 75' conference in Johannesburg, Giancarlo de Carlo raised concerns about the task of producing 'finite' objects and called for designers to choose 'to be on the side of the users … and leave the ambiguity of working for them and face the harder task of working with them'.[1]

Architecture, even in its most simplistic form of object-centred building, cannot really live in isolation. Rather, it must engage with diverse networks and balance different actors, functions and materials. Particularly today, the complexity of architecture is such that it requires an impressive and unprecedented epistemological pluralism, with a nuanced range of tones and atmospheres. In instances where the social, cultural and economic conditions are fragmented and diverse the task becomes more complicated still. Thus, in order to avoid the risk of being lost in translation, the ramifications of cultural models for the built environment need to be built into – and communicated in – the visual and spoken languages that we use to understand the symbolic nature of forms.

Fortunately, over the last four decades or so, architecture's growing interest in the social sciences has enabled a multiplicity of audiences to relate to projects that were previously marginalised by canonical, western hierarchies. Ecology's expanded role, as a metaphor in the conceptualisation of schemes, has also provided a fillip to wider engagement. The important recognition that a single design philosophy is no longer capable of providing adequate responses has given rise to the open, experimental culture that informs these two projects, empowering both users and designers alike.

Traditions

In the intertwining, interdependent stories told by the different persons involved in the Thread Cultural Centre in Senegal and the Floating School in Nigeria, we have a body of knowledge that is primarily oral, and that has a tendency, when written, to be unproblematically interpreted as fact. We need to bear this in mind in our role as observers, and remember Jean-Paul Bourdier's call to engage in a 'critical practice concerned among other things with ... breaking the monotony, if not the oppression, of standardisation'.[2]

A good case in point is the parametric modelling of the sinuous thatch roof of the Thread Cultural Centre, a contemporary reinterpretation of the traditional impluvium houses of the Casamance region of southern Senegal. Aware of the difficulty of graphically representing the richness of the material assembly, and of the fact that local builders would need some latitude in translating a drawing into built form, the architect did not develop a full set of detailed construction plans. In order to have the roof built, Dr Ba, who doubled as contractor/construction manager, relied instead on the indigenous knowledge of an experienced roof assembler, Gregoire Bienquench, a Bassari from the Kédougou region. The aesthetically captivating result is owned by the community it serves, since it reflects their involvement in every step of the construction process. The material nature of the roof intrinsically provides a 'living' dimension to the structure; moreover, through its periodic maintenance the bonds between the villagers and the centre are continually renewed.

Irregularities in this context are not picturesque, or poetic licences, but rather represent and embody the multifaceted lives of the people who inhabit the spaces. The incidental perception of these relations is what constructs an ecology of factors. In its efforts to examine projects holistically, the Aga Khan Award for Architecture emphasises the discovery of the pluralities on the ground, including all sorts of irregularities. Thus the agents behind the projects, and their stories, can no longer be bystanders in the narrative. However snatched or chaotic their lives might be, they are the reality around which the fictional narrative of architecture as an ordering discipline is constructed.

Accumulations

In Makoko, the Floating School's success in terms of capturing attention, putting the community on the map, has tended to relegate to the background the question of how well it actually functions as a school. After the collapse of the prototype structure in June 2016, the jury is still out on its effectiveness as a space for learning. In some ways, this is an apt reminder of the discourse around the colonial tension between issues of 'becoming' and 'being' that Taiaiake Alfred captured so well.[3] Descriptions of Makoko as an apparently confused and unstructured mess remain superficial, failing to engage with its true ordering principle: an ecosystem based on the economy of exchange and recycling that lives – or at the very least hopes to live – in balance with its territory.

However, we need to note here that the funding model for the Floating School – with financial support provided by an international development agency – placed severe constraints on its operation, since it did not directly engage the inhabitants in the processes of the design and construction. What has emerged is a disjuncture between 'knowing' – in this particular case, knowing how to conceptualise and build a floating A-frame timber structure – and 'doing' things, such as operating and maintaining a watercraft moored in a tropical lagoon. The old paradigms are not put into question by the conceptual distance between the two; rather, the original asymmetrical relation of donors and receivers is maintained.

The community's capacity to autonomously generate and organise space – and its resilience even after the collapse of the structure – is perhaps the kind of situation that Giovanni Arrighi and Beverly J Silver had in mind when they concluded their *Chaos and Governance* with a warning that the transformation of the modern world into a commonwealth of civilisations was going to be 'drastic and painful'; indeed, we could not even be certain that this transformation 'would eventually result in a commonwealth rather than in mutual destruction'.[4] In the face of the growing environmental, economic and social inequality that communities like Makoko so vividly portray, we are reminded that it is in places such as this that the future of the planet itself is being played out.

Alternatives

Different in many ways, the stories of Makoko and Sinthian both point to the utility – even the urgency – of abandoning the simplistic contraposition of bottom-up and top-down architecture. In both cases the architects found themselves operating in conditions where they were perceived as outsiders by the community, and had to rely on local mediators to establish a dialogue with the users of the buildings. The projects are an important reminder of the need to create the preconditions for a reciprocal understanding, particularly before building in situations of scarce resources. This is not just a plea for the (re)discovery of the power of participation. It implies a questioning of the system of architectural education, to allow for a greater recognition of models of co-production.

Without pretending to formulate a general theory, the ecosystemic narrative that emerges from fragments of interaction with a plurality of actors and their cultures suggests the possibility for architecture to be looked at – even if not entirely understood – through multiple, inevitably incomplete and hybrid sources of information, made up of rifts and tensions. This conjecture seeks to play a transformative role in an experimental, co-produced education that will hopefully unlock the potential of new generations of architects and their clients. In the meantime, we may be assured that many more speculative and subversive experiments, of the kind described here, will be required to determine new paradigms and to instil confidence in the civic legitimacy of the discipline within an increasingly fragile world order.

1 Giancarlo de Carlo, 'What is housing?', in M Lazenby (ed), *Housing People* (Johannesburg: Ad Donker, 1977), 38.
2 Jean-Paul Bourdier, 'Reading Tradition', in JP Bourdier and N Al Sayyad (eds), *Dwellings, Settlements and Tradition: Cross-Cultural Perspectives* (Lanham, MD: University Press of America, 1989), 36.
3 Taiaiake Alfred, *Being and Becoming Indigenous: Resurgence against Contemporary Colonialism* (Melbourne: Narrm Oration, 2013).
4 Giovanni Arrighi and Beverly J Silver, *Chaos and Governance in the Modern World System* (Minneapolis: University of Minnesota Press, 1999), 286.

Guelmim School of Technology

Guelmim, Morocco

Guelmim School of Technology grew out of the efforts of the Moroccan government and the Ibn Zohr University of Agadir to decentralise higher education and give students in remote areas the chance to go to university without having to move to one of the big cities – Agadir, Casablanca, Marrakesh. The repetitive, pared-down buildings that make up the school are simultaneously modern – blocks pierced by projecting window frames, louvers and narrow openings – and a tribute to the traditional buildings of the region. Known as the 'Gateway to the Desert', Guelmim is located on the edge of the Sahara in semi-arid, southern Morocco, with the Anti-Atlas Mountains to the north. Its proximity to the Atlantic serves to moderate its climate, though fluctuations in temperature can still be quite extreme.

For ease of navigation, the campus has a linear, branching organisation. The two main areas are arranged along a north–south axis around a series of courtyards and shaded walkways made of metal and timber elements. Spaces are easily differentiated by function: the southern part of the complex contains administrative offices and shared facilities such as the library, lecture hall and infirmary, while the northern section contains most of the teaching rooms and social spaces, such as the student cafeteria.

The three architects developed their own environmental brief in response to the context, ensuring that the campus is well adapted to the desert climate. The interior spaces are carefully organised to maximise natural ventilation and lighting, and are painted and furnished in white, with terrazzo flooring made from local stone. Green areas – formed of native plants, able to thrive in the dry climate – fill the spaces between the buildings, which are further integrated into their surroundings through the ochre colour of their facades. The rough render of these reinforced-concrete facades – reminiscent of traditional architecture – captures the light on the surfaces in a particularly expressive way. Indeed, the play of light and shadow is the only decorative element of the exteriors.

Client
Ibn Zohr University, Agadir, Morocco:
Omar Halli, president

Architects
Agence Saad El Kabbaj Architecte: Saad El Kabbaj, principal, Casablanca, Morocco
Agence Driss Kettani Architecte: Driss Kettani, principal, Casablanca, Morocco
Agence Mohamed Amine Siana Architecte: Mohamed Amine Siana, principal, Casablanca, Morocco

Structural Engineer
Bepol, Ouarzazate, Morocco:
Hassan Amgoune, director general
Jamaa Balil, project manager

Laboratory
LPEE, Agadir, Morocco:
Bachir El Cherkaoui, director general
Lahcen Errguibi, project manager

Technical Control Office
Dekra, Agadir, Morocco:
Imad Khamlichi, director general
Mustapha Essaadi, project manager

Construction Company
Zerkdi et fils, Agadir, Morocco:
Abdallah Zerkdi, director general
Houssine Idhamou, project manager

Project Data
Total site area: 45,000 m^2
Total built area: 6,883 m^2
Cost: 5,730,000 USD
Commission: January 2008
Design: January 2008–January 2010
Construction: March 2010–September 2011
Completion: October 2011

Saad El Kabbaj – Driss Kettani – Mohammed Amine Siana
Born in 1978 in Casablanca, Saad El Kabbaj studied at the Ecole Nationale d'Architecture in Rabat, Morocco, where he graduated in 2003, interspersing his studies with work experience abroad. He opened his office in Casablanca in 2005 and works especially on residential projects.

Born in 1978 in Fez, Driss Kettani spent his childhood in Côte d'Ivoire before coming to Morocco in 1996 and studying at the Ecole Nationale d'Architecture in Rabat, where he graduated in 2003. After some collaborative work, he opened his office in Casablanca in 2005, working on housing, office projects and design.

Born in 1979 in Casablanca, Mohamed Amine Siana graduated from the Ecole Nationale d'Architecture in Rabat, Morocco, in 2004. From 2000 he worked with different architects both at home and abroad before opening his own office in Casablanca in 2005. He works on a range of projects including interior design, housing, health and design.

In parallel with their own projects, the three architects have collaborated on some important commissions. They won the competition for the Polydisciplinary Faculty of Taroudant in 2006, which was completed in 2010, and were awarded second prize in the competition for the Casablanca Grand Stadium with Portuguese partners Risco and LDS in 2011. They are currently at work on other educational projects, such as the Lycée Lyautey restructuring in Casablanca. Other projects include the Laayoune School of Technology and some mixed-use developments.

The Guelmim School of Technology won the 2015 Archmarathon Award in the educational category, and their work has been featured in exhibitions in New York, Milan, Melbourne, Paris and elsewhere. The architects have taught in the summer workshop Wave 2014 and at IUAV in Venice, and have given lectures in Morocco, Italy, Lebanon and France.

Websites
www.drisskettani.com
www.saadelkabbaj.com

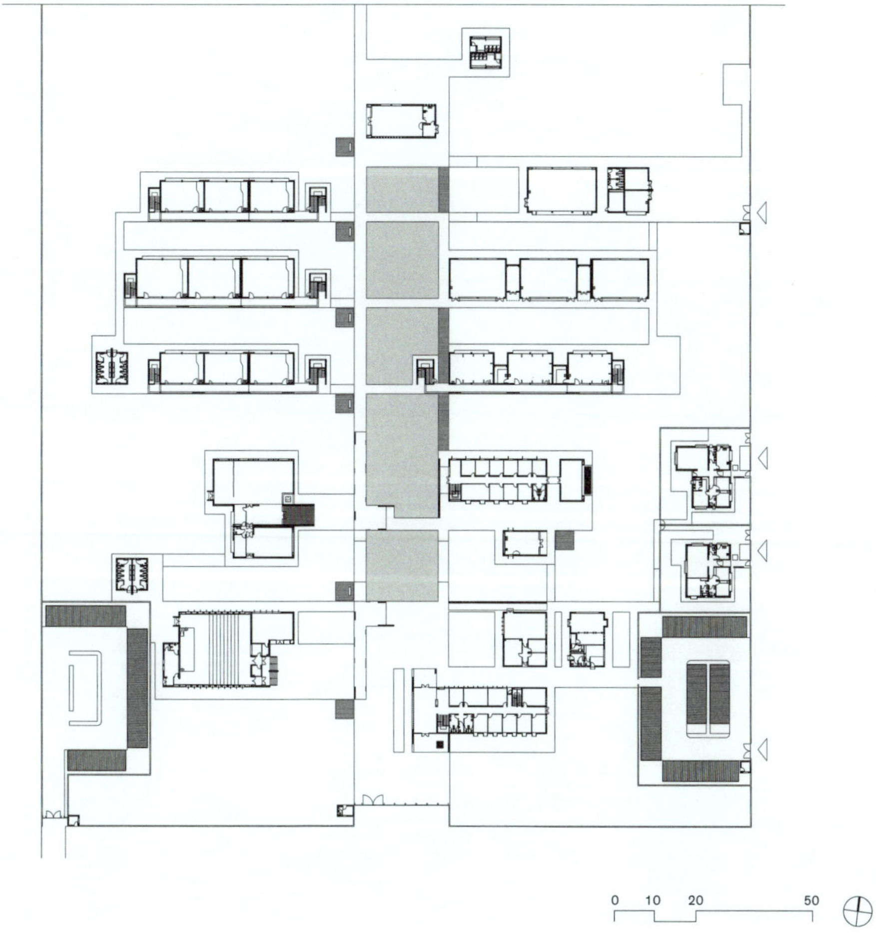

Royal Academy for Nature Conservation

Ajloun, Jordan

The Royal Academy for Nature Conservation is set in the Ajloun highlands, in a rolling landscape of farmland and forests of oak interspersed with pistachio, carob and wild strawberry trees. In addition to their agricultural value, these hills are also the source of the Anjara limestone found in much of Jordan's traditional architecture.

On being commissioned to design the academy – a centre promoting environmental education and ecotourism – the architect's first step was to have the building moved from the proposed site within the Ajloun forest reserve. Rather than clear protected woodland, he persuaded the client to build over a nearby abandoned quarry.

The irregular design of the limestone-clad facade follows the contours of the quarry – quite literally so, as the architect drew a line on the vertical surface of the rock to guide the stonemasons at the start of the work. The building rises from this line, transitioning almost seamlessly from bedrock to masonry construction – a mass of rough-textured local limestone. The south-facing facade is pierced by very small windows; solar gain is mitigated by tapered concrete louvers – vertical blade-like cracks shearing into zero width. On the other side of the building, diamond-shaped columns in exposed reinforced concrete are angled 45 degrees over the trees in order to create voids under the terraces and, most importantly, to reduce the impact of the construction on the surrounding environment.

Access to the academy is by way of a 30 m bridge, a hybrid structure of stone and reinforced concrete. The interior of the building is divided into two zones – an educational area and a restaurant/kitchen – organised around a central entrance lobby. The main circulation corridor is infilled with tapered stone blocks – smaller versions of the tapered concrete louvers inserted into the exterior windows. When the skylight above the corridor throws sunlight down over these blades of stone it creates a play of light that evokes the rough textures of the quarry outside.

From a construction point of view, it is partly ambiguous whether this is a building that is made from the materials of the quarry, or a quarry that is trying to make an architecture.

Client
Royal Society for the Conservation of Nature, Amman, Jordan:
Hasan Osama, construction manager

Architect
Khammash Architects, Amman, Jordan:
Ammar Khammash, principal
Osama Odeh, Deema Assaf, architects

Engineer
Al-Arabi Group Consulting, Amman, Jordan:
Mohammed Halawani, senior structural engineer
Mohammad Odeh, structural engineer

Contractor
Sami Al-Hafi Establishment for Contracting, Amman, Jordan

Geo-thermal System
GEO Contracting Company, Amman, Jordan

Electric
Energy Management Services (EMS), Amman, Jordan

Project Data
Total site area: 156,780 m^2
Total project area: 3,600 m^2
Building footprint area: 1,950 m^2
Cost: 3,912,000 USD
Commission: April 2008
Design: April 2008–September 2011
Construction: May 2011–April 2014
Completion: May 2014

The Royal Society for The Conservation of Nature:
The Royal Society for The Conservation of Nature (RSCN) is a non-governmental organisation that aims to create, manage and act as advocate for a national network of protected areas to conserve Jordan's biodiversity and support local community development, while promoting wider public support and action for the protection of the natural environment within Jordan and neighbouring countries. Under the patronage of Her Majesty Queen Noor, RSCN was established in 1966 with His Majesty the late King Hussein as Honorary President. RSCN has the mission of protecting wildlife and wild places. Thus it is one of the few national organisations in the Middle East with such a public service mandate. As a result of its pioneering conservation work, the RSCN has achieved international recognition and acclaim.

Ammar Khammash
Ammar Khammash is the principal architect and founder of Khammash Architects in Amman. He received his bachelor's degree in architecture from the University of Southwestern Louisiana in 1986, and attended the post-graduate programme in ethno-archaeology at the Institute of Archaeology and Anthropology in Al-Yarmouk University (1987–1988). Khammash has undertaken a wide range of residential, cultural and renovation work, sustainable tourism, research and planning, as well as 'destination design' projects. These include the Royal Academy for Nature Conservation in Ajloun (2014), Feynan Eco-Lodge in Wadi Feynan (2002) and the Wild Jordan Nature Center in Amman (2001).

Ammar Khammash is well established as an expert in Jordan's cultural and natural heritage and has launched a number of websites on Jordan's flora, geology and heritage. His expertise spans different disciplines including history, geology, archaeology, ecology, botany, ethnography and socio-economics. He is the author of a number of publications including *Notes on Village Architecture in Jordan* (1986). He is also an established painter in Jordan and has held more than 20 art exhibitions; his art work has been published in *Ancient Landscapes: The Landscape Paintings of Ammar Khammash* (2009).

Website
www.rscn.org.jo
www.khammash.com

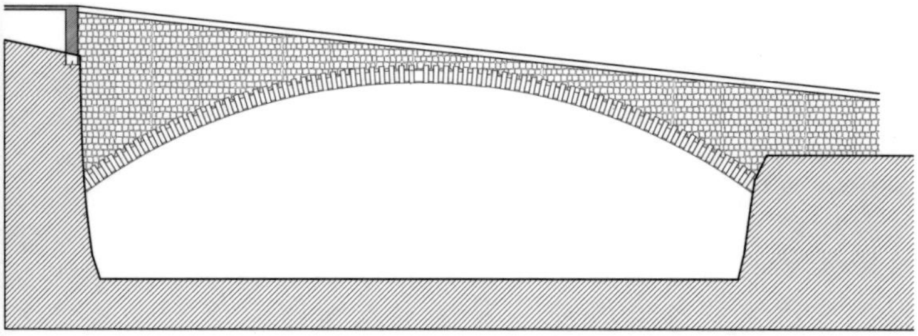

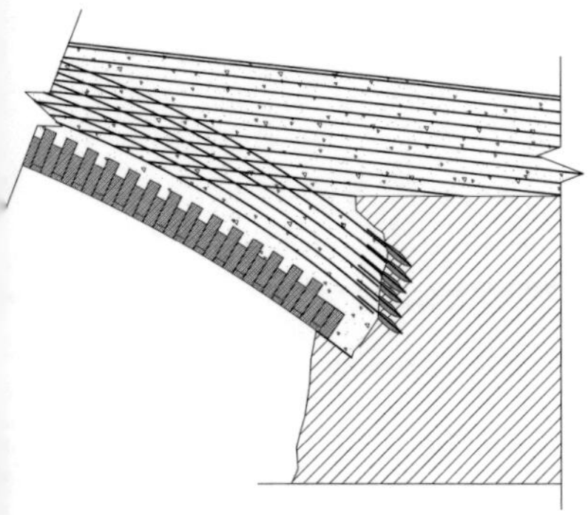

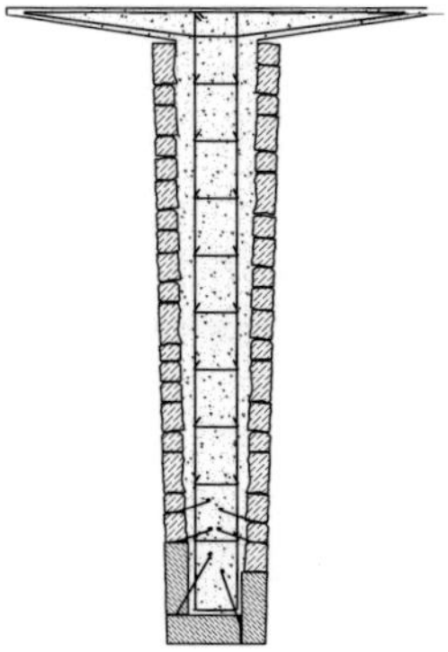

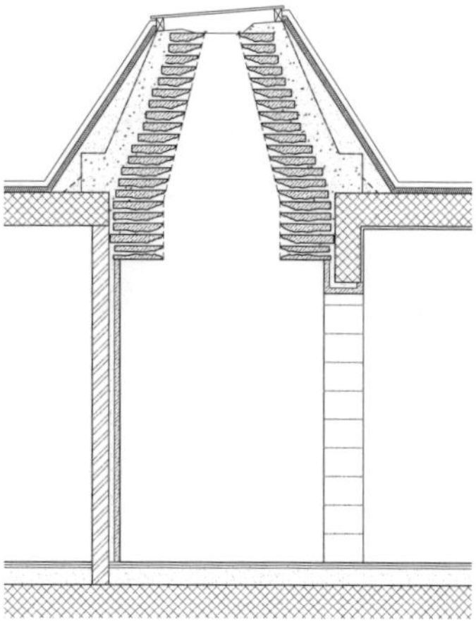

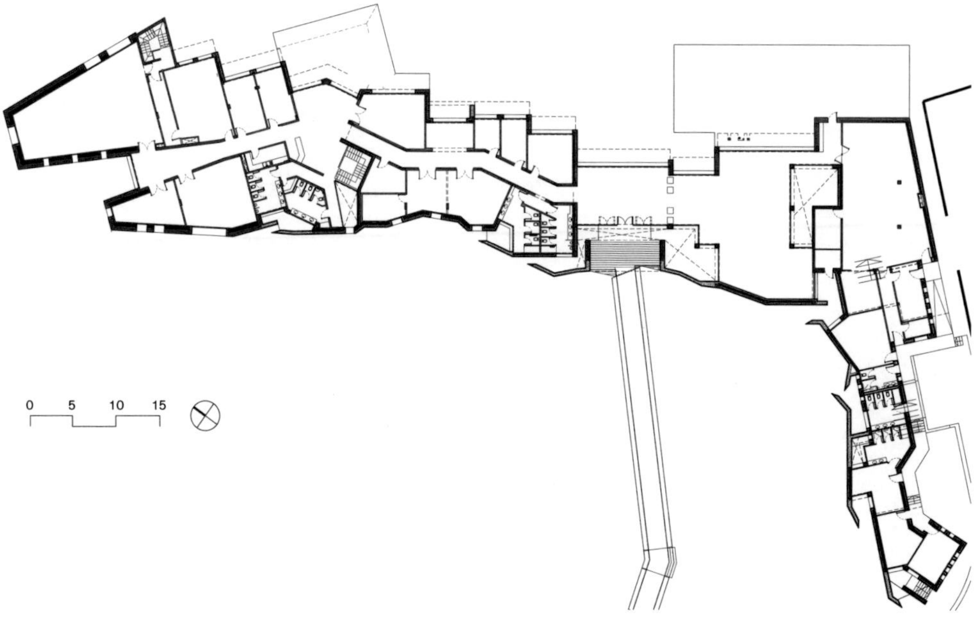
0 5 10 15

Ceuta Public Library

Ceuta, Spain

Ceuta has a character all of its own, as a quasi city-state bordering Morocco but belonging to Spain, from which it is separated by the Straits of Gibraltar. And the city's public library is equally distinct. In addition to the typical functions of a modern library and cultural venue, it integrates within its structure important archaeological remains from a fourteenth-century Marinid city, built by Muslims retreating from the Iberian Peninsula.

The design of the structure developed out of extensive discussions with the site archaeologist, who identified three points where it would be acceptable to penetrate the ground, as the historical layers had disappeared. The columns were constructed on micro-piles: thick and wall-like, they set up a visual connection with the structure of the archaeological site – two parallel streets lined with houses. A viewing gallery allows the whole of the site to be appreciated from above, effectively 'in plan'. Taking advantage of the height differential in the sloping terrain, a second entrance at the back of the building, at mezzanine level, provides direct access for visitors wanting to see the archaeological exhibition rather than use the library.

The library has many different components – reading rooms, auditorium, activity rooms, multimedia areas, bookstore, terrace and outdoor reading area. To unify them all, the architects developed the idea of a 'veil'. The whole of the building above ground level is covered with aluminium panels, perforated both to filter the harsh glare of the sun and to provide views out. At an early stage, the architects drew viewpoints to identify the best outlooks – over the city and towards the Mediterranean – and made these an integral part of the design. Views to the building were also an important consideration, given its visibility on the sloping site. The lines created by the aluminium panels reflect the gradients of the streets, while the warm beige colour of the concrete base connects the library with the surrounding rocky landscape. The veil, wrapping around all sides equally, hides utilitarian functions such as ducts. At night the face of the building changes, as the veil becomes partially transparent.

Clients
Spanish Ministry for Culture, Madrid, Spain:
Amando Cuellas, general manager for infrastructure works

Municipality of Ceuta, Spain:
María Isabel Deu del Olmo, cultural manager

Architect
Paredes Pedrosa Arquitectos, Madrid Spain:
Angela Garcia de Paredes, Ignacio Garcia Pedrosa, partners
Lucía Guadalajara, Álvaro Rábano, Clemens Eichner, Álvaro Oliver, Guiomar Martín, Eva Urquijo, Ángel Camacho, Ignacio Cordero, Blanca Leal, Roberto Lebrero, project team

Technical Control
Luis Calvo, Madrid, Spain
Antonio Zoido, Ceuta, Spain

Structural and Mechanical Engineering
Gogaite SL/JG Ingenieros, Madrid, Spain:
Alfonso Gómez Gaite, Alfonso Redondo Gómez, partners

Archaeological Survey
Muncipality of Ceuta, Spain:
Fernando Villada Paredes, director of excavations
José Suárez, Elena Ortuño, Estrella Arcos, archaeologists

Project Data
Site area: 1,050 m^2
Total combined floor area: 6,759 m^2
Total cost: 12,000,000 USD
Commission: September 2007
Design: October 2007–May 2008
Construction: February 2010–April 2013
Occupancy: December 2013

Paredes Pedrosa Arquitectos
Ángela García de Paredes and Ignacio Pedrosa graduated in 1982 from the Escuela Técnica Superior de Arquitectura de Madrid (ETSAM), where they are now professors in the architectural design department. They are also visiting professors and critics at other universities as well as at the IUAV in Venice. After graduating, they worked with José García de Paredes until 1990, when they established Paredes Pedrosa, a firm mainly dedicated to competitions and projects for public cultural buildings. Their built works include La Olmeda Roman villa and public libraries in Ceuta and Córdoba, cultural buildings that integrate archaeological remains, and they have also undertaken specific interventions in historical buildings with heritage interest. Their work has been recognised with important awards such as Spain's Gold Medal for Achievement in the Fine Arts in 2014, the Spanish Architecture Award 2007 and, among others, the AADIPA European Award for Architectural Heritage 2015, the Eduardo Torroja Award 2014, an Honourable Mention for the Piranesi Prix de Rome 2014, the Gold Medal International Prize for Sustainable Architecture 2012, Special Mentions for Europa Nostra, 2006 and 2010, and the AR+d Award for Emerging Architecture 1999.

Website
www.paredespedrosa.com

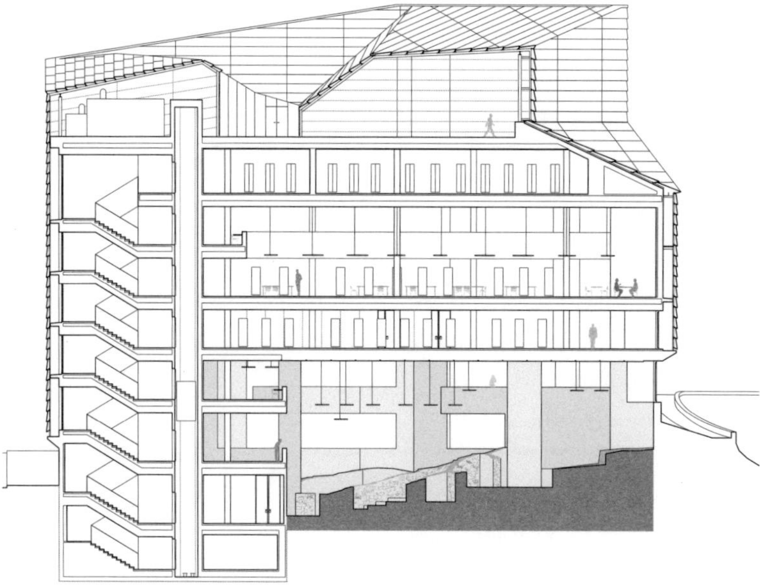

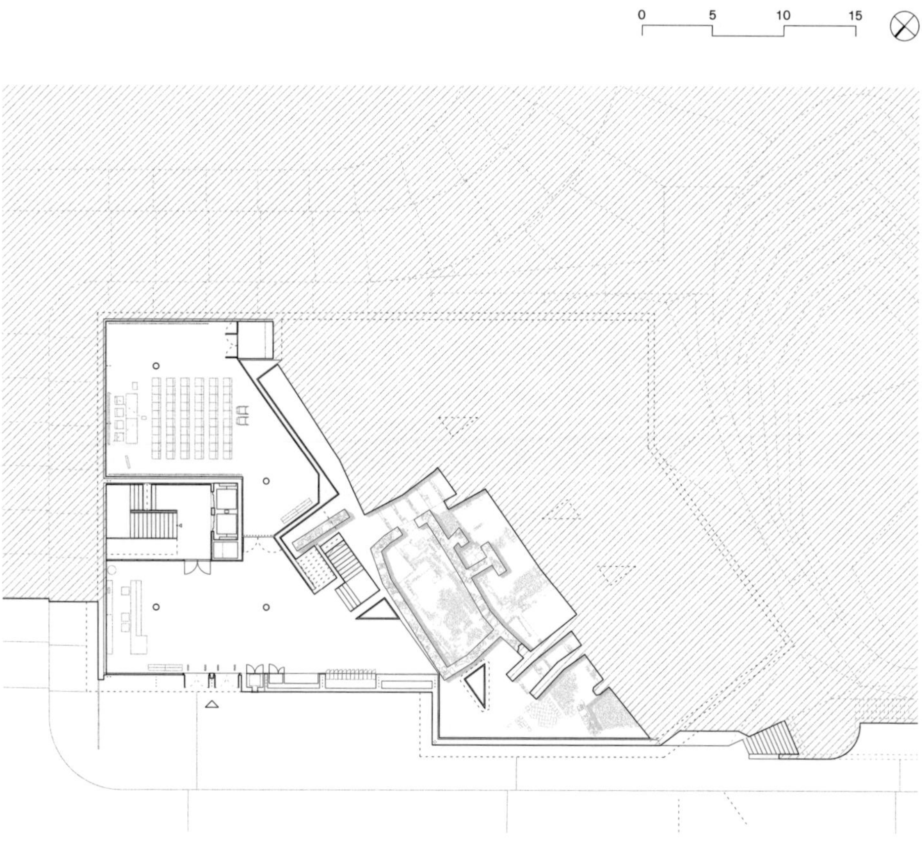
0
5
10
15

TECHNOLOGY

What role can technology play in promoting the cause of architecture within Muslim societies? In addition to being used to improve the quality of architecture, from concept to implementation – from the use of computers to new techniques of construction – technology has also served as the means for framing a new approach to the question of representation and appearance. The Doha Tower in Qatar continues some of the geometric strategies first shown at the Institut du Monde Arabe in Paris, but here applied to a high-rise structure – an approach that enables the building to be contemporary while recalling the tradition of geometric patterns that is so deeply embedded within the local culture. Similarly, the King Fahad National Library in Saudi Arabia uses the concept of a deep 'lightweight' facade to provide a geometrically intricate exterior. The use of technology here produces a Janus-faced facade – representational on the outside, and providing shade from direct sunlight in the interior.

Doha Tower

Doha, Qatar

Doha Tower is one of the most distinctive landmarks in the Qatari capital. Designed by French architect Jean Nouvel, the 46-storey office building was commissioned by Sheikh Saud bin Mohammed Al Thani in the early 2000s as part of a larger strategy to give the city a modern urban skyline inspired by international cities like Hong Kong – but with an Islamic cultural twist. The design is based on a round-tower typology – not unlike Nouvel's Torre Agbar in Barcelona – covered with an aluminium outer facade. Like a mashrabiyya, this brise-soleil is defined by an abstract, geometric pattern. Butterfly-shaped aluminium tiles at four different scales are overlaid along the facade in response to solar conditions. The varying density of the layers – ranging from 25 per cent opacity on the north elevation to 60 per cent on the east and west – has a sculptural effect, producing subtle changes in the geometry and the external appearance of the screen.

Combined with the slightly reflective glass curtainwall that makes up the inner facade, the aluminium screen creates a play of light and shade in the interior office spaces. Large open-plan floors, with 3 m ceilings, are generated through the application of an innovative diagrid (diagonal grid) structure of round, reinforced-concrete columns located in the perimeter of each office floor. The dome at the top of the tower has a crisscrossing lattice-steel structure distinct from the diagrid columns.

The design of the interior reflects the client's desire for a cool industrial aesthetic, with its combination of grey fair-faced concrete walls and galvanised steel flooring and ceiling. A further dose of drama is added by the large interior atrium, which houses eight glass lifts reaching 112 m to the 27th floor.

The long gestation of the project, combined with the technological precision of the design, called for a close collaboration between the Qatari clients, the French architects, the Chinese structural engineers and fabricators and local distributors and contractors, making Doha Tower a truly international work.

Client
Saud bin Mohammed bin Ali bin Abdullah bin Jassim bin Mohammed Al Thani, Doha, Qatar

Client Representative
Hassan Al Duhaimi, Doha, Qatar

Architect
Ateliers Jean Nouvel, Paris, France:
Jean Nouvel, principal
Hafid Rakem, Ingrid Menon, project managers
Marie-Hélène Baldran, Vincent Laplante, Emmanuel Biard, Antoine Bordenave, Gian Luca Ferrarini, Lina Ghotmeh, Nick Gilliland, Eva Grimard, Nicolas Laisne, Marie Maillard, Stefan Matthys, Barbara Sajgalikova, Carmen Salinas, Anna Sans, Anne Traband, Elodie Vadepied, Camille Vidal, Nives Voinov, Nabila Zerrouki, Anna Voeller, project team

Consultants – Design Stage
Terrell International, Paris, France:
Peter Terrell, structural and MEP consultant

BCS SA Cormondreche, Neuchâtel, Switzerland:
Philippe Bissat, facade consultant

Avel Acoustique, Paris, France:
Jean Paul Lamoureux, acoustic consultant

JP Molé SAS, France:
Jean-Pierre Molé, parking consultant

Europtima, quantity surveyor, Paris, France

Socotec International, security consultant, Montigny-le-Bretonneux, France

Pluriconsult, kitchen consultant, Fresnes, France

MTC Surveys, surveyor, Doha, Qatar

Local Architect
Arab Engineering Bureau, Doha, Qatar:
Ibrahim Al Jidah, local architect

Consultants – Construction
Gardiner & Theobald International, Doha, Qatar:
Chris Mentell, Quantity Surveyor

Gleeds Gulf Engineering Consultants, Construction Management, Doha, Qatar:
Douglas Bayley, project manager
Mamoon Atout, construction manager

Dar Al Handasa, Construction Management, Doha, Qatar:
Hani Akkawi, project manager

Socotec International, Dubai, UAE:
Alain Sabah, structural engineering

Ian Banham & Associates, Abu-Dhabi, UAE, mechanical engineering

Lighting Design
Aik, Paris, France:
Yann Kersale, lighting consultant

Landscaping
Ingénieurs et Paysages, Versailles, France: Jean-Claude Hardy, landscape consultant

Contractor
China State Construction Engineering Corporation Ltd, Beijing, China:
Guo Haizhou, Project Manager

Sub-contractors
Hebei Jinhuan Steel Structure Engineering Co Ltd, steel structure, Hebei, China
Zhu Hai King Glass Engineering Co Ltd, aluminium facade and glass, Zhuhai, China
Samko, MEP Contractor, Doha, Qatar

Project Data
Diameter: 45 m
Height: 231.5 m
Total built area: 110,000 m^2
Total site area: 13,000 m^2
Cost: 186,850,000 USD
Commission: 2002
Design: July 2002–July 2003
Construction: August 2004–March 2012
Completion: 2012

Jean Nouvel
Jean Nouvel ranked first in the entrance examination to the Ecole Nationale Supérieure des Beaux-Arts in Paris in 1966 and obtained his degree in 1972. Assistant to the architect Claude Parent and influenced by urban planner and essayist Paul Virilio during his studies, he started his first architecture practice in association with François Seigneur in 1970. Soon afterwards, he became a founding member of 'Mars 1976', the movement whose purpose was to establish links between people and decision makers, and, subsequently, was a founder of the Syndicat de l'architecture. His strong stances and provocative opinions on contemporary architecture in the urban context together with his unfailing ability to inject originality into all the projects he undertakes have formed his international image.

In 1989 his Institut du Monde Arabe in Paris was the recipient of an Aga Khan Award for Architecture and, in 2000, Nouvel received the Lion d'Or of the Venice Biennale. In 2001 he received three of the highest international awards: the Royal Gold Medal of the Royal Institute of British Architects (RIBA), the Praemium Imperial of Japan's Fine Arts Association and the Borromini Prize for the Culture and Conference Centre in Lucerne. He was the recipient of the prestigious Pritzker Prize in 2008. In France, he has received many awards including the Gold Medal of the French Academy of Architecture, two Equerres d'argent and the National Grand Prize for Architecture. His current firm, Ateliers Jean Nouvel, is one of the largest architectural practices in France, active in the fields of architecture, urban design, landscape design as well as industrial and interior design.

Website
www.jeannouvel.com

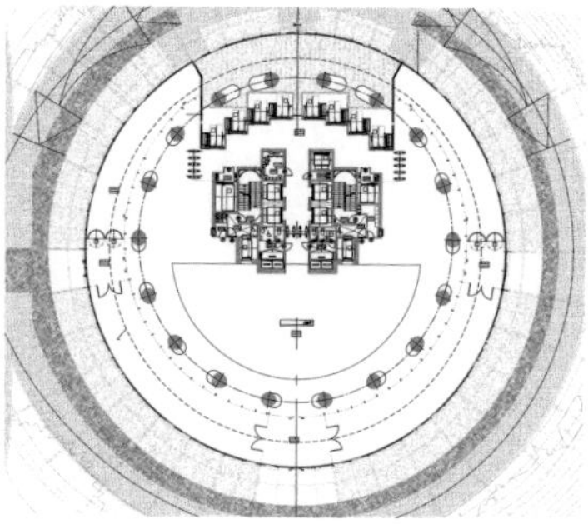

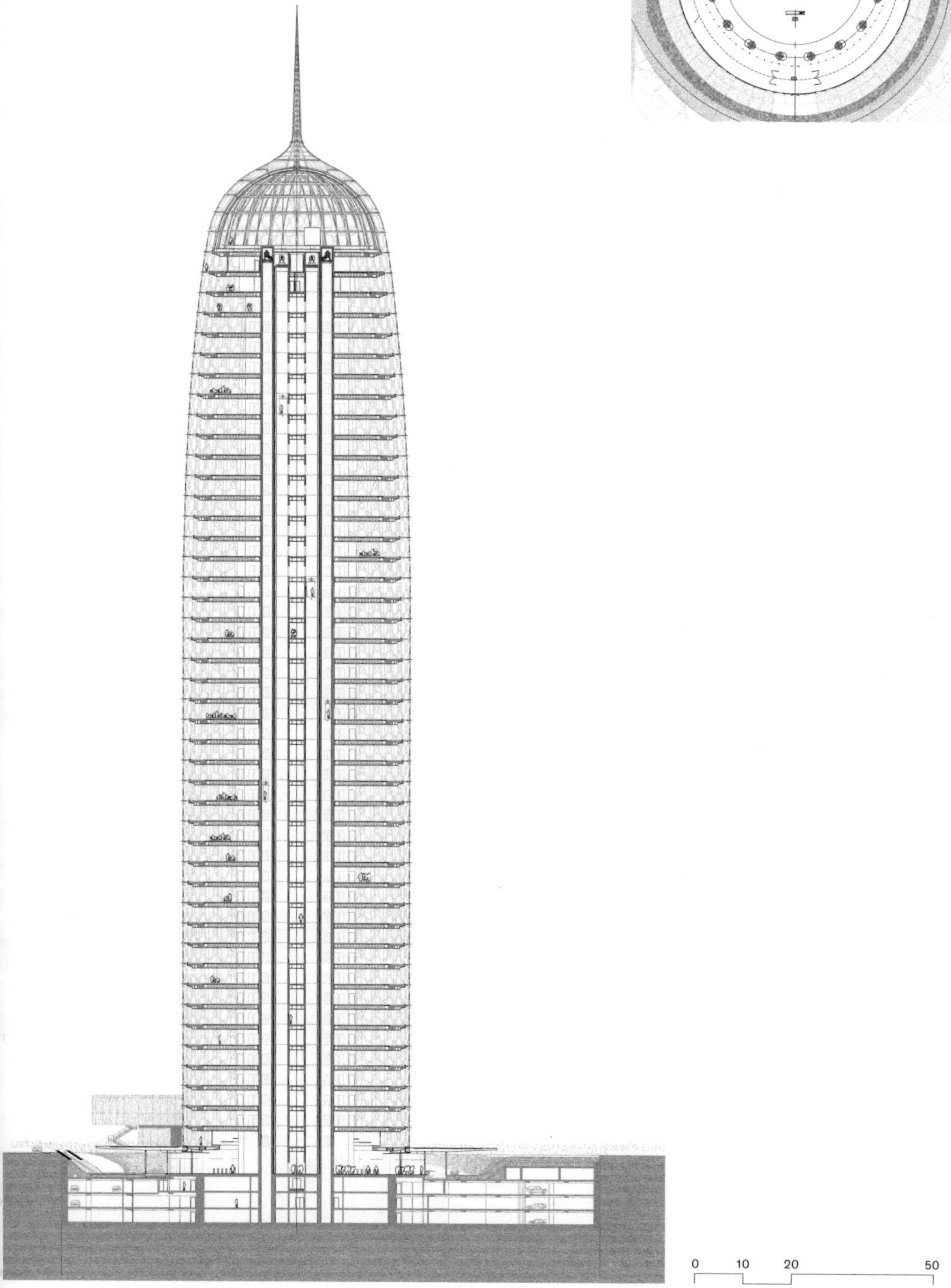

0
10
20
50

Doha Tower, Doha, Qatar

Deep Skin Triumphs

Hanif Kara

As architects today step up to embrace the potential of advances in technology, they often find themselves meeting technologists coming the other way, in search of some meaning greater than 'making as the only reality'. The shortlist for this 13th Award Cycle does not escape that paradoxical state. In all of the 19 projects we can trace, in varying degrees and combinations, the intricate relationship and tension between two contemporary cultures – a tension most vividly expressed in the building's 'skin'. On the one hand, there is the 'representational' – the rationale of everyday life, dominated by cultural values and traditions that are not easily converted into technical terms (in architecture this strand often starts from phenomenology); on the other, the 'technological' – the rationale of an autonomous horizon that sanctions anonymity and challenges the adequacy of representation (in turn, this often starts from science).

Going beyond this tension, the selection of projects for the Award is guided by a rigorous, tried-and-tested process that draws our attention to the whole range of issues faced by those involved in shaping the built environment today – whether as clients, designers, constructors or inhabitants of the space. The projects may be tall, small, curved, flat or broad: we are encouraged to look beyond the themes of aesthetics or tectonics to consider how the architects engage with the key goal of improving the quality of life while responding to the growing challenges posed by rapid urbanisation, population growth and environmental change.

How, then, do we evaluate this engagement? And how do we connect these projects to the idea of plurality which in the context of the Award is a framework of ethical and cultural values articulated through architecture.[1] As an avowed technologist, my innate tendency is to fall back on professional responsibility quantified by efficient closed systems based on criteria such as cost, constructability or performance. That approach is not effective here. To address this complex task I would therefore propose that the full shortlist of 19 is treated as a 'bundle', ensuring that no project is reduced to a single 'architectural type', since the work eludes such neat categorisation. Try, for example, to compare the Superkilen urban park in Denmark with the Tabiat Pedestrian Bridge in Iran using the familiar framework of 'public space': one is on the ground and used by the diaspora of 60 cultures, the other is suspended in the air and predominantly serves a single community. To avoid the temptation to theorise a singular aspect of the architecture, we need to acknowledge the projects as a set of exemplars. In that way, the plurality of the bundle offers a convenient multiplicity of ideas – some intended by their designers, others most likely not. From this, we can methodically find the transformational impact of these ideas and reverse-engineer the bundle to derive a notional pluralistic model (figure 1). At the heart of this model lies 'architectural memory and history' and its multiple connections to other fields, from philosophy to politics and economics.

To further elaborate the bundle and, more precisely, the winning projects, we can then return to the element that most vividly illustrates the tension in contemporary practice – the skin of the building. It is possible to individuate the full range of the skin, from its narrowest interpretation – patina – to its deepest – the core of the project. Here, to some extent, the skin takes on mixings propagated by the current dissolution of boundaries – geographical, political, economic, technological, aesthetic and cultural.

Let's start, then, by sampling some soundbites extracted from video interviews with the architects provided by the Award. The quotes are grouped in accordance with material or technique.

Figure 1: A notional pluralistic model of useful concepts derived from the shortlist of the Award 2016

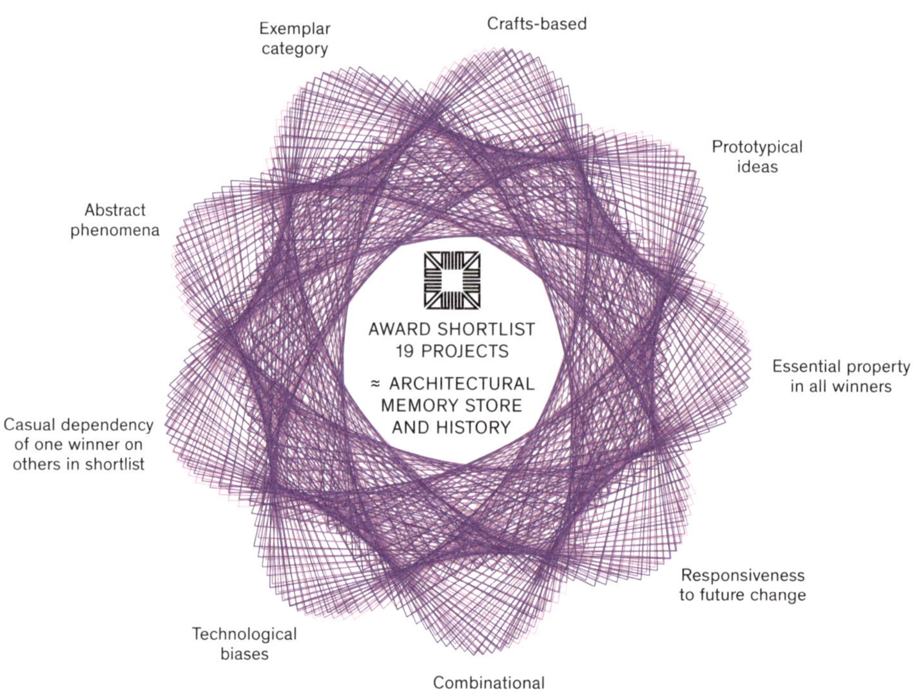

Set 1: Skin as low-technology **craft-based** materials and techniques

'It's naturally ventilated and, interestingly, the brickwork is load-bearing.'
Marina Tabassum, Bait ur Rouf Mosque, Bangladesh

'The idea behind using stone is that it's local and ages well.'
Amer Kammash, Royal Academy for Nature Conservation, Jordan

'When you touch these amazing bricks you get the feeling that you are touching a valuable carpet with a set of knots.'
Alireza Mashhadi Mirza, 40 Knots House, Iran

'Broken forms of beautiful handmade bricks ...'
Kashef Chowdhury, Friendship Centre, Bangladesh

'A diagonal offset brick keeping dust and rain out, but allowing light in ... We took care to use local material differently.'
Toshiko Mori and Jordan MacTavish, Thread Cultural Centre, Senegal

Set 2: Skin as **primary structural** system (potential redundancy in performance compared to sets 1 and 3)

'People like to stay on it'; 'Even though it's full of steel it feels like I am walking in a forest'.
Leila Araghian and a visitor, Tabiat Pedestrian Bridge, Iran (exposed steel tubes)

'The whole building is conceived as heavy building.'
Saleem Jalil, Issam Fares Institute, Lebanon (exposed reinforced concrete)

'[It's] split into three areas: a red square, a black square and a green park on the ground.'
Nanna Gyldholm Møller, Superkilen, Denmark (patina only)

Set 3: Skin as **high-technology** materials and techniques

'[It's] covered with one large roof – that's why you see a tensile structural fabric screen that provides shading on the outside: we tried to create something technological with the vernacular.'
Thomas Lücking, King Fahad National Library, Saudi Arabia

'A glass cylinder protected by a mashrabiyya with different levels of cover (differentiated opacity) ... We used aluminium and worked with tension and restraint.'

Jean Nouvel, Doha Tower, Qatar

'That's why the aluminium panels are not horizontal, but parallel to the street.'

Angela Garcia, Ceuta Public Library, Spain

Proportionately the capital costs of skins are significant in any project (figure 2), but skins are responsive to change: facades can easily be replaced, not so foundations. And as figure 3 shows, set 3 – high-technology materials and techniques – consume a large amount of energy in their manufacture compared to set 1 (craft-based materials and techniques).

What observations can we make based on these samples? What makes the skin so relevant to how we perceive the work of architecture as a whole? The theoretician and curator Stephan Trüby reminds us that the facade – the face of a building – participates in processes of visual categorisation: 'The facade is so powerful – like a face it triggers an almost Pavlovian response, a cascade of judgements about hierarchy and value ... modern attempts to destabilise the hierarchy perhaps need a few more hundred years to embed themselves in the western brain.'[2] And others, such as the journalist Virginia Postrel, go even further in describing how the aesthetic imperative taps into deep human instincts: 'Valuable goods and services are worth more in attractive wrappings is one way of looking at substance and its relationship to surface.'[3]

In reality, the last two decades have seen a significant erosion of the architectural profession as responsibility for the design of facades has increasingly been surrendered to other, more technologically advanced disciplines. Against this troubled background, the 'deep skin triumphs' of the Award shortlist are to be celebrated. In each case, the richness of the skin is the outcome of the architect's successful negotiation and mediation of the variegated tensions at work in the projects. It is to be hoped that, as a set of exemplars, this bundle will inspire others to reclaim a more certain role for the architect and bring about a renewed attachment to task that lies at the very core of the discipline – so averting a wreckage for future designers of the world.[4]

1 See Homi Bhabha, 'From Public Space to Public Sphere' in Mohsen Mostafavi (ed), *Architecture is Life: Aga Khan Award for Architecture* (Zurich: Lars Müller, 2013). For a perspective from outside the AKAA, see also Aaron Olko, 'Pluralism in Architecture', paper for 'The Digital Turn', Southern California Institute of Architecture, Fall 2012.
2 'Facade' in Rem Koolhaas et al, *Elements* (Venice: Marsilio Editori, 2014).
3 Virginia Postrel, *The Substance of Style: How the Rise of Aesthetic Value is Remaking Commerce, Culture and Consciousness* (New York: Harper Collins, 2003).
4 Richard E Susskind and Daniel Susskind, *The Future of the Professions* (Oxford: Oxford University Press, 2015).

Figure 2: Embodied energy: energy usage in manufacturing of skin materials

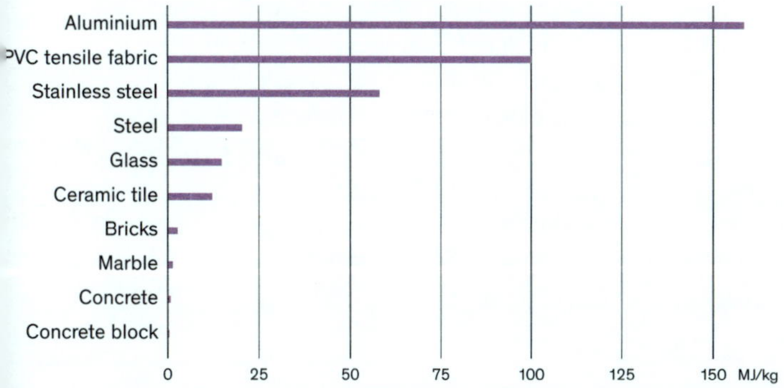

Figure 3: Capital cost of skin proportion

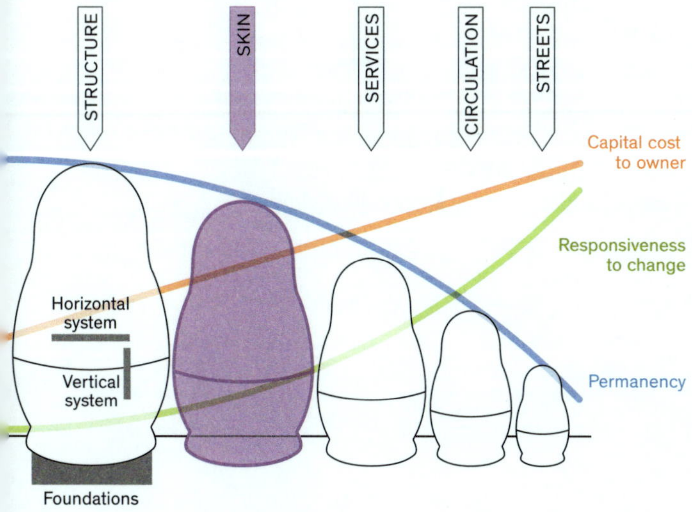

King Fahad National Library

Riyadh, Saudi Arabia

Riyadh's new King Fahad National Library is an impressive architectural, technological and urban undertaking. Enveloping the original 1980s building on the site, it doubles the capacity of the library while providing a public plaza of equal size – a generous gift of open, pedestrian-friendly space in the Kingdom of Saudi Arabia's vehicle-centric capital. The horizontal plane of the plaza defines its boundaries solely through its slight elevation above the surrounding asphalt. Its granite paving, identical to the flooring of the building's lobby, creates a sense of continuity between the two.

The preservation of the 1980s cruciform, dome-topped building – now completely wrapped within the new structure – echoes the remit of the national library itself, which is to preserve and document cultural traditions including, in this instance, the memories of a place. The original library now holds the closed stacks, and the interior as a whole is organised over three floors. The ground level is for circulation and reception (books arrive in boxes to be sorted and catalogued), the second floor for administration. The top floor contains the central reading room, a spacious semi-public space that ties the new steel and glass extension to the entire former roof of the existing building. More than a simple room, this is a reading 'landscape' with ample daylight and sun-protected transparency.

But the most remarkable feature of the King Fahad National Library is perhaps the cladding of the facade. Rhomboidal textile awnings shade the building from direct sunlight while allowing for a maximum of transparency – with views looking in, at the inner workings of the library, as well as out, towards the urban plaza and the city skyline. A reinterpretation of traditional tent structures, the white membranes are supported by a three-dimensional, tensile-stressed steel cable structure. All elements of the facade can withstand the extremes of Riyadh's climate, from the peak of the summer (50°C in the shade) to below zero during winter evenings. Significantly reducing energy consumption and increasing thermal comfort, the library incorporates layered ventilation and floor cooling, appearing here for the first time in the Arab world.

Clients
Arriyadh Development Authority, Riyadh, Saudi Arabia:
Abdulrahman Al-Sari, director of urban and cultural programme
Waleed Alekrish, construction project director
Khalid Al-Hazani, director of architecture
Thomas Ciolek, senior architect

King Fahad National Library, Riyadh, Saudi Arabia:
Mohammed Al-Rashed, director general
Mohammed Al-Husaini, general manager IT

Architect
Gerber Architekten International GmbH, Dortmund, Germany:
Eckhard Gerber, general manager and owner
Thomas C Lücking, general manager and design director

Landscape Architects
Gerber Architekten, Dortmund, Germany
Kienle Planungsgesellschaft Freiraum und Städtebau GmbH, Stuttgart, Germany

Local Partner and Engineer
SaudConsult, Riyadh, Saudi Arabia:
Khurram Karamat, vice president
Nadeem Sheik, senior structural engineer

Mechanical and Electrical Engineer
Drees & Sommer Group-Pan, Stuttgart, Germany:
Peter Mösle, partner
Jurenka Michael, senior mechanical engineer
Ralf Wagner, senior electrical engineer

Structural Engineer
Bollinger + Grohmann, Frankfurt am Main, Germany:
Manfred Grohmann, chairman
Mark Fahlbusch, partner

Site Supervision Team
Arriyadh Development Authority, Riyadh, Saudi Arabia:
Ahmed Al-Drees, structural engineer
Anas Al-Mousa, structural engineer
Yasser Al-Qadi, mechanical engineer

Saudconsult, Riyadh, Saudi Arabia:
Fawzi Al-Toom, site manager
Mohammed Sulaiman, architect

Gerber Architekten International GmbH:
Thomas C Lücking, general manager and design director

Main Contractor
Saudi Bin Laden Group, Jeddah, Saudi Arabia:
Fraih Haddad, project manager
Mohammed Faisal, project architect

Steel Contractor
Ali Tamimi Sons Co, Riyadh, Saudi Arabia:
Eid Tamimi, CEO

Project Data
Total site area: 59,558 m^2
Old library area: 27,547 m^2
Ground floor area: 14,618 m^2
Combined floor area: 86,632 m^2
Cost: 84,370,000 USD
Commission: March 2003
Design: January 2004–August 2006
Construction: December 2008–November 2013
Completion: December 2013

Gerber Architekten
Gerber Architekten is an award-winning architecture firm based in Dortmund, Germany, with offices in Hamburg, Berlin, Shanghai and Riyadh. The company was founded by Professor Eckhard Gerber in 1966 and currently employs around 170 staff. The firm follows a generalist approach, taking responsibility for a project from the design idea all the way to construction and handover. It is committed to creating an architecture that combines functionality with timelessness and longevity, thus creating projects that are sustainable by design. Over the past 50 years, Gerber Architekten has realised numerous projects in all fields of architecture, national and international. Recent projects include the multiple award-winning King Fahad National Library and the iconic Olaya Metro Station in Riyadh, Saudi Arabia.

Websites
www.kfnl.gov.sa
www.gerberarchitekten.de

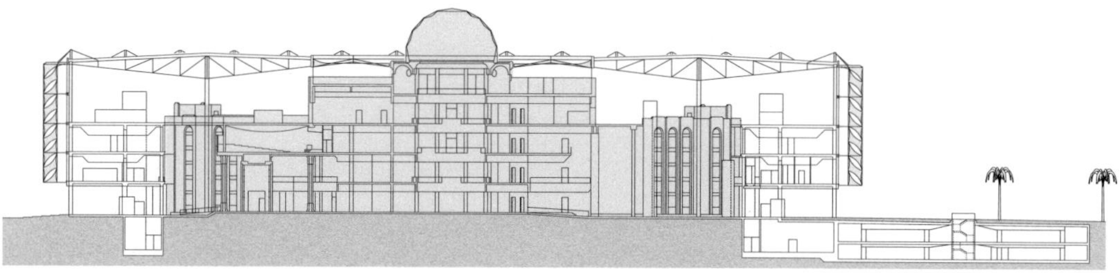

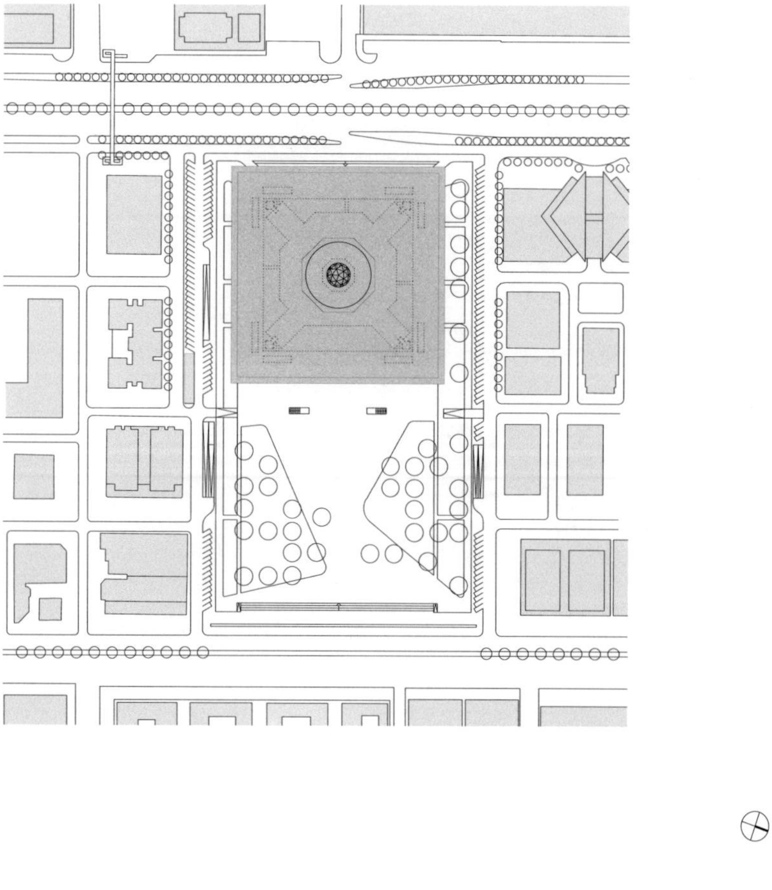

On Environmental Responsiveness and Technology Integration

Hossein Rezai

The integration of technology into our built environment is essential because of its potential not just to mitigate but to heal the damage wrought by our ever-increasing demands on the planet. Minimisation of heat gain through building orientation, the use of screens and mashrabiyyas, behavioural change, the reduction of embodied and operational carbon footprints – all are important and essential responses to the challenges faced in the ever-expanding built environment. But in themselves, these passive steps are not nearly enough. They cannot reverse the damage that has already been caused, nor can they put a stop to it in the future.

To roll back the damage already inflicted on the environment, particularly over recent decades, technology is our only effective tool. Only the application of technology can lead to a carbon-positive future where our buildings and bridges are transformed into power stations, producing more energy than they consume.

In this light the crucial issues of environmental responsiveness and technology integration should be seen as the two sides of the same coin, as intrinsic parts of the same whole. Throughout the years the Aga Khan Award for Architecture has encouraged and rewarded such projects and initiatives.

Of the 348 projects presented to the Master Jury for the 13th cycle, 32 displayed notable environmental awareness in their construction or sustainable energy- and water-management practices. In the initial review of entries, initiatives such as the IRIS project in Beirut and the LIFT project in Bangladesh caught the attention of the jury.

Located by the sea, the IRIS project consisted of two 'eyelids' that opened and closed with the movement of the tides, in the process harnessing the energy of the waves and converting it into electricity. The installation looked somewhat futuristic, and indeed it turned out to be so. Certain practical aspects of the rather interesting idea had not been sufficiently resolved to make the installations permanent enough for inspection by the review team.

The LIFT House combined renewable and water-saving features for affordable housing with an innovative approach to floating structures. While its central 'core' remained firmly anchored in the ground, its two wings of accommodation were designed to float on water in the event of flooding. Again, the idea was commendable, but it transpired that the actual prototype house had faced a number of problems.

Other entries integrated technological excellence into their design to achieve sustainability goals. Khamsa House is a low-embodied carbon structure. The construction incorporates bricks made with compressed earth from the site and a cementitious binder. The house also deploys a combination of renewable generation systems – both wind and solar sources – to achieve an operational zero-energy status. During times of low occupancy, excess energy can be exported to the national grid, benefiting the surrounding areas as part of a decentralised energy network.

Another zero-energy building, the Masdar Institute, is entirely powered by solar energy. The inflated ETFE panels incorporated into its facade, though lightweight, provide a highly effective solution to controlling extreme variations in heat and temperature. Recognition of these efforts could help to make the use of such innovative materials more mainstream.

The Mauritius Commercial Bank, the first BREAAM-certified building in the Southern Hemisphere, incorporates highly sophisticated technology in a different manner. Its Building Management System includes sensors which track the path of the sun, monitoring the intensity of solar radiation and cloud cover and adjusting the indoor climate to achieve the optimum efficiency for the building zones.

Technology can be used not only in construction and operation, but also in design optimisation. Siemens' Middle East headquarters employed computer algorithms to determine the precise size, shape and positioning of its facade elements and sun-shading devices to minimise solar radiation while maximising light penetration.

The use of parametrics takes the integrated design and modelling process to the next level, helping to achieve the most efficient use of materials. Though it may not have been derived from such rigorous parametric analyses, the variable intensity of the double-skin shading device of the Doha Tower reflects this principle. In turn, the multilayered glass and stone facade of KAPSARC Community Mosque speaks of similar aspirations.

The Ford Otosan R&D Centre uses a different technological innovation: that of transforming elements within a building to allow for multiple functions, a strategy that can effectively reduce the building footprint. Such developments will hopefully also make it possible for other infrequently occupied spaces – such as stadia or conference halls – to have more varied usage in the future.

The Park Royal Hotel in Singapore, with its lush, vegetated terraces, takes urban greenery to new heights. By providing a wide range of habitats, the plants are improving biodiversity in a dense urban environment and positively affecting the microclimate of the neighbourhood as a whole. The successful establishment of such an extensive high-rise landscape depends both on rigorous studies of the local micro-ecology and on the appropriate use of technology.

Such bold ideas deserve recognition and encouragement. Environmental sustainability is not limited to active and visible measures such as low-energy buildings powered by photovoltaic panels. Rather, it can be demonstrated using a multitude of techniques and approaches across a whole range of scales. Carbon footprints can be reduced by selecting cutting-edge low-carbon materials and processes such as cement-free concrete or Precast, Prefabricated Volumetric Construction (PPVC), or by integrating parametric or simulation-driven forms that lead to passive design excellence. The use of locally appropriate materials and technology has historically been beneficial in urban development, but today's development agendas require a more sophisticated and global approach.

Looking at past Award recipients from the 1995 to 2013 cycles, four buildings in particular stand out for the way they address their environmental impact: the Salam Centre for Cardiac Surgery, Bibliotheca Alexandrina, Moulmein Rise Residential Building and Menara Mesiniaga.

The Salam Centre for Cardiac Surgery and Bibliotheca Alexandrina are both focused on material reuse and operational energy-effectiveness. Moulmein Rise takes passive design and climate responsiveness as the basis for its design and form, both in its external massing and its internal layouts and details. And Menara Mesiniaga set a new trend in environmental responsiveness and technology integration at the time it was designed and developed – some 20 years ago.

The brief of the Aga Khan Award for Architecture clearly favours a congruent approach to the fundamentals of environmental protection, sustainability and technical integration. A wide range of projects is submitted in each cycle. However, it is fair to say that environmental credentials generally do not feature in a rigorous and consistent manner in all of the entries. The past emphasis on the strong cultural and social aspects of the architecture may have created a belief that environmental and technological innovation is not what the jury members are looking for when they are making their selection.

This is not so. While questions of social equity and integration are indeed important, they are by no means the only considerations. It is to be hoped that future cycles of the Award will attract a larger pool of such interesting and technologically rich projects and in turn reward them for their innovative aspects as much as for their architectural and social merit.

Beyond Function

Dominique Perrault

Though diverse, the projects included in this volume all share one trait in common: they see the context as having an essential function in defining architecture. This is a specific role that goes beyond the notion of functionalism set out by the modern movement in the twentieth century. Rather, in establishing a relation of use between a building and its environment, it proposes to create spaces that can accommodate functions other than those enumerated in the programme of construction.

We should note here that the importance of a building within its context does not increase in direct proportion to its scale. For example, the very small library in the hutong in an old part of Beijing creates a micro-landmark that speaks, through its use, of the life of the neighbourhood. In order to intensify activity, this building densifies the urban fabric, in stark contrast to the rational planning approach, which would demolish an old neighbourhood in order to replace it with something completely new.

At the other end of the scale we have the Tabiat Pedestrian Bridge in Iran, an immense (XXL) piece of infrastructure. This is not so much a simple bridge that links two parks or sides of a highway as a whole bundle or network of bridges that weave together, transforming at certain points into belvederes or promenades – uses that do not generally fall within the ambit of a generic bridge. Here too, new surfaces have been created to embrace the diversity of urban life.

A new type of public space is being created by the architecture of the buildings. As proof of this we have the Bait ur Rouf Mosque in Dhaka, Bangladesh, with its very precise and delicate organisation in which the vestibule, with its little colonnades, defines an architectural place in between the exterior public space and the mystic heart of the building. Likewise, in the Friendship Centre in rural northern Bangladesh, the public space extends over the top of the building, creating a kind of rooftop park. Akin to an archaeological ruin, the building is submerged in the landscape, offering a garden in place of a facade. So, once again, these two buildings go beyond the simple definition of function to propose new surfaces in the urban fabric or rural landscape.

In Beirut this interplay between the existing and the new finds a spectacular and convincing expression. The Issam Fares Institute has a very strong architectural presence, yet curiously its footprint is extremely minimal. This form frees the ground and creates a great window onto the landscape, in the process establishing a very positive relationship with the more traditional buildings around it: rather than aggressively enclosing the courtyards and gardens, the modern building opens up the campus. Here too a respect for the use of the existing ground creates a new ground, which floats like a cantilever over the campus.

In conclusion, we might say that contemporary architecture is more concerned with the geographical situation of a building than was perhaps the case in the recent past. A historical analysis of the context no longer seems an adequate basis on which to elaborate an architectural statement that fulfils the needs of both society and the environment.

'Beyond function' becomes 'beyond architecture'.

The transverse nature of the sharing economy points to the importance of horizontality – of extending the terrain – as a strategy for the sustainable development of cities and landscapes. Verticality in itself cannot ensure the quality of the environment. This new, more sensitive approach is engendering more open attitudes, as the strict respect for function gives way to unexpected, improbable, unprecedented uses – something absolutely vital for society today.

2016 Award Steering Committee

His Highness the Aga Khan
Chairman

David Adjaye
Architect; Principal, Adjaye Associates, London, UK

Mohammad al-Asad
Architect and Architectural Historian; Founder and Chairman, Center for the Study of the Built Environment, Amman, Jordan

Francesco Bandarin
Architect and Urban Planner; Assistant Director General, UNESCO, Paris, France

Hanif Kara
Structural engineer; Design Director and Co-Founder, AKTII, London, UK, and Professor in Practice of Architectural Technology, Graduate School of Design, Harvard University, Cambridge, USA

Kamil Merican
Architect; Principal Designer and CEO, Group Design Partnership, Kuala Lumpur, Malaysia

Azim Nanji
Social Scientist; Special Advisor, Aga Khan University, Nairobi, Kenya

Gülru Necipoğlu
Architectural Historian; Director, Aga Khan Program for Islamic Architecture at Harvard University, Cambridge, USA

Brigitte Shim
Architect; Partner, Shim-Sutcliffe Architects, Toronto, Canada and Professor, John H Daniels Faculty of Architecture, Landscape and Design, University of Toronto, Canada

Yu Kongjian
Landscape Architect; Founder and Dean, Graduate School of Landscape Architecture, Peking University, Beijing and Founder and Principal Designer, Turenscape, Beijing, China

Farrokh Derakhshani
Director of the Award

2016 Award Master Jury

Suad Amiry
Architect and Writer; Founder, Riwaq Centre for Architectural Conservation, Ramallah, Palestine

Emre Arolat
Architect; Founder, EAA-Architects, Istanbul, Turkey

Akeel Bilgrami
Philosopher; Sydney Morgenbesser Professor of Philosophy, Columbia University, New York, USA

Luis Fernàndez-Galiano
Architect; Editor, *Architectura Viva*, and Professor, School of Architecture, Madrid, Spain

Hameed Haroon
Publisher; Chief Executive Officer of Pakistan Herald Publications Ltd, Karachi, Pakistan

Lesley Lekko
Architect; Head, Graduate School of Architecture, Johannesburg University, Johannesburg, South Africa

Mohsen Mostafavi
Architect and Educator; Dean and Alexander and Victoria Wiley Professor of Design, Graduate School of Design, Harvard University, Cambridge, USA

Dominique Perrault
Architect; Founder, Dominique Perrault Architecture, Paris, France

Hossein Rezai
Structural Engineer; Director of Web Structures, Singapore

2016 Award On-Site Review Members

Azra Akšamija
Artist and Architectural Historian; Associate Professor, MIT Program in Art, Culture and Technology, Cambridge, USA

Tomà Berlanda
Architect; Director, School of Architecture, Planning and Geomatics, University of Cape Town, South Africa

Nondita Correa Mehrotra
Architect; Principal, RMA Architects, Mumbai, India, and Boston, USA

Ahmad Djuhara
Architect; Principal, djuhara+djuhara and President, Indonesian Institute of Architects, Jakarta, Indonesia

Seif El Rashidi
Architectural Historian and Cultural Heritage Specialist, London, UK

Abdul-Halim Jabr
Architect and Urban Design Consultant; Co-Founder and Consultant UNIT44, Beirut and Professor, Holy Spirit University of Kaslik, Mount Lebanon, Lebanon

Gökhan Karakuş
Architecture Critic, Theorist and Designer; Director, Emedya Design, Istanbul, Turkey

Hoshiar Nooraddin
Architect and Urban Planner; Associate Professor, School of Architecture and Interior Design, Canadian University of Dubai, UAE

Hassan Radoine
Architect Planner; Professor and Director, Ecole Nationale d'Architecture, Rabat, Morocco

Bekim Ramku
Architect and Urbanist; Director, OUD+Architects and Director, Prishtina Architecture Week, Prishtina, Kosovo

Mamadou Jean-Charles Tall
Architect; Co-Director, J&T Architectes et Associés, and President of the Board, Collège universitaire d'architecture, Dakar, Senegal

Recipients of the Aga Khan Award for Architecture 1980–2016

2016
Bait ur Rouf Mosque, Dhaka, Bangladesh
Friendship Centre, Gaibandha, Bangladesh
Superkilen, Copenhagen, Denmark
Micro Yuan'er Children's Library and Art Centre, Beijing, China
Tabiat Pedestrian Bridge, Tehran, Iran
Issam Fares Institute, Beirut, Lebanon

2013
Salam Centre for Cardiac Surgery, Khartoum, Sudan
Rehabilitation of Tabriz Bazaar, Tabriz, Iran
Revitalisation of Birzeit Historic Centre, Palestine
Rabat-Salé Urban Infrastructure Project, Rabat and Salé, Morocco
Islamic Cemetery, Altach, Austria

2010
Wadi Hanifa Wetlands, Riyadh, Saudi Arabia
Revitalisation of the Hypercentre of Tunis, Tunisia
Madinat al-Zahra Museum, Cordoba, Spain
Ipekyol Textile Factory, Edirne, Turkey
Bridge School, Xiashi, Fujian Province, China

2007
Samir Kassir Square, Beirut, Lebanon
Rehabilitation of the City of Shibam, Wadi Hadhramaut, Yemen
Central Market, Koudougou, Burkina Faso
University of Technology Petronas, Bandar Seri Iskandar, Malaysia
Restoration of Amiriya Complex, Rada, Yemen
Moulmein Rise Residential Tower, Singapore
Royal Netherlands Embassy, Addis Ababa, Ethiopia
Rehabilitation of the Walled City of Nicosia, Cyprus
School in Rudrapur, Dinajpur, Bangladesh

2004
Bibliotheca Alexandrina, Alexandria, Egypt
Primary School, Gando, Burkina Faso
Sandbag Shelter Prototypes, various locations worldwide
Restoration of Al-Abbas Mosque, Asnaf, Yemen
Old City of Jerusalem Revitalisation Programme, Jerusalem
B2 House, Bükhüsun Village, Ayvacik, Turkey
Petronas Towers, Kuala Lumpur, Malaysia

2001
New Life for Old Structures, various locations, Iran
Aït Iktel, Abadou, Morocco
Kahere Eila Poultry Farming School, Koliagbe, Guinea
Nubian Museum, Aswan, Egypt
SOS Children's Village, Aqaba, Jordan
Olbia Social Centre, Antalya, Turkey
Bagh-e-Ferdowsi, Tehran, Iran
Datai Hotel, Pulau Langkawi, Malaysia

1998
Rehabilitation of Hebron Old Town, Hebron, Palestine
Slum Networking of Indore, Indore, India
Salinger Residence, Selangor, Malaysia
Lepers Hospital, Chopda Taluka, India
Tuwaiq Palace, Riyadh, Saudi Arabia
Alhamra Arts Council, Lahore, Pakistan
Vidhan Bhavan, Bhopal, India

1995
Restoration of Bukhara Old City, Bukhara, Uzbekistan
Conservation of Old Sana'a, Sana'a, Yemen
Hafsia Quarter II, Tunis, Tunisia
Khuda-ki-Basti Incremental Development Scheme, Hyderabad, Pakistan
Aranya Community Housing, Indore, India
Great Mosque and Redevelopment of the Old City Centre, Riyadh, Saudi Arabia
Menara Mesiniaga, Kuala Lumpur, Malaysia
Kaedi Regional Hospital, Kaedi, Mauritania
Mosque of the Grand National Assembly, Ankara, Turkey
Alliance Franco-Sénégalaise, Kaolack, Senegal
Re-Forestation Programme of the Middle East Technical University, Ankara, Turkey
Landscaping Integration of the Soekarno-Hatta Airport, Cengkareng, Indonesia

1992
Kairouan Conservation Programme, Kairouan, Tunisia
Palace Parks Programme, Istanbul, Turkey
Cultural Park for Children, Cairo, Egypt
East Wahdat Upgrading Programme, Amman, Jordan
Kampung Kali Cho-de, Yogyakarta, Indonesia
Stone Building System, Dar'a Province, Syria
Demir Holiday Village, Bodrum, Turkey
Panafrican Institute of Development, Ouagadougou, Burkina Faso
Entrepreneurship Development Institute of India, Ahmedabad, India

1989
Great Omari Mosque, Sidon, Lebanon
Rehabilitation of Asilah, Morocco
Grameen Bank Housing Programme, various locations, Bangladesh
Citra Niaga Urban Development, Samarinda, Indonesia
Gürel Family Summer Residence, Çanakkale, Turkey
Hayy Assafarat Landscaping, Riyadh, Saudi Arabia
Al-Kindi Plaza, Riyadh, Saudi Arabia
Sidi el-Aloui Primary School, Tunis, Tunisia
Corniche Mosque, Jeddah, Saudi Arabia
Ministry of Foreign Affairs, Riyadh, Saudi Arabia
National Assembly Building, Sher-e-Bangla Nagar, Dhaka, Bangladesh
Institut du Monde Arabe, Paris, France

1986
Social Security Complex, Istanbul, Turkey
Dar Lamane Housing, Casablanca, Morocco
Mostar Old Town, Mostar, Bosnia-Herzegovina
Al-Aqsa Mosque, al-Haram al-Sharif, Jerusalem
Yaama Mosque, Yaama, Tahoua, Niger
Bhong Mosque, Rahim-Yar Khan, Pakistan
Shushtar New Town, Shushtar, Iran
Kampung Kebalen Improvement, Surabaya, Indonesia
Ismaïlliya Development Projects, Ismaïliyya, Egypt
Saïd Naum Mosque, Jakarta, Indonesia
Historic Sites Development, Istanbul, Turkey

1983
Great Mosque of Niono, Niono, Mali
Sherefudin's White Mosque, Visoko, Bosnia-Herzegovina
Ramses Wissa Wassef Arts Centre, Giza, Egypt
Nail Çakirhan House, Akyaka Village, Turkey
Hafsia Quarter I, Tunis, Tunisia
Tanjong Jara Beach Hotel and Rantau Abang Visitors' Centre, Kuala Terranganu, Malaysia
Résidence Andalous, Sousse, Tunisia
Hajj Terminal, King Abdul Aziz International Airport, Jeddah, Saudi Arabia
Tomb of Shah Rukn-i-'Alam, Multan, Pakistan
Darb Qirmiz Quarter, Cairo, Egypt
Azem Palace, Damascus, Syria

1980
Kampung Improvement Programme, Jakarta, Indonesia
Pondok Pesantren Pabelan, Central Java, Indonesia
Ertegün House, Bodrum, Turkey
Turkish Historical Society, Ankara, Turkey
Mughal Sheraton Hotel, Agra, India
Conservation of Sidi Bou Saïd, Tunis, Tunisia
Rüstem Pasha Caravanserai, Edirne, Turkey
National Museum, Doha, Qatar
Ali Qapu, Chehel Sutun and Hasht Behesht, Isfahan, Iran
Halawa House, Agamy, Egypt
Medical Centre, Mopti, Mali
Water Towers, Kuwait City, Kuwait
Courtyard Houses, Agadir, Morocco
Inter-Continental Hotel and Conference Centre, Mecca, Saudi Arabia
Agricultural Training Centre, Nianing, Senegal

Acknowledgements

Photo Credits
Iwan Baan: 173–175, 177, 180–181, 183, 188–189, 219, 220–221, 224–225, 269, 274–275; Barzin Baharlouei: 20–21, 129–131, 133–135, 138–141, 146–147, 233–235, 238–239, 253–255, 258–259; Didier Boy de La Tour: 261, 263; Hamid Reza Darajati: 136–137; Cemal Emden: 22–23, 153–155, 157–163, 168–169, 199–201, 204–205, 207–209, 212–213, 241–243, 246–247, 291–293, 296–297, 299–301, 304–305, 309–311, 314–315, 323–325, 328–329; Torben Eskerod: 173; Murat Germen: 330; CNES/Astrium, Google Earth: 287; Jens Lindhe: 182; Dragør Luftfoto: 14–15; Zhang MingMing: 79, 88–89; Neo Spot: 262, 266–267; NLÉ: 270–271, 283–285, 288–289; Prithula Prosun: 331; Ieva Saudargaite: 332; Su Shengliang: 87, 94–95; Kristian Skeie: 46–47, 178–179; Skyshot Pte Ltd: 333; Rajesh Vora: 18–19, 24–25, 59–61, 63–69, 74–75, 99, 100–101, 103–109, 115; Hou Xinjue: 84–85; Zhang Yifan: 87; Wang Ziling: 16–17, 80–81, 83, 86; ZAO/standardarchitecture: 91

Drawings
All drawings are supplied by the architects.

Additional illustrations, videos and information about the 2016 projects and other background material is available at www.akdn.org/architecture

The activities of the 13th cycle of the Aga Khan Award for Architecture (2014–16) have been completed in large part due to the contribution and support of the following people:

Aga Khan Trust for Culture
Luis Monreal, general manager
Sirwan Abdulaziz, accounting officer
Shiraz Allibhai, deputy director
Karine Labry, administrative assistant
Amanda Monney, senior executive assistant
Lobna Montasser, media and documentation officer
Van Nguyen, senior IT coordinator
Sandrine Niesor, senior assistant
Sam Pickens, deputy director, AKDN communications
Thê-Hông Tang-Lam, digital production officer

Award Secretariat
Farrokh Derakhshani, director
Céline Bouchacourt Martenot, executive assistant
Nadia Siméon, award coordinator

Regional Coordinators
Fay Cheah, South-East Asia
Khadija Jamal-Saban, Pakistan
Bekim Ramku, Balkans
Berend van der Lans, East Africa
Bahrom Yusupov, Central Asia

Documentation Assistance
Nuha Ansari
Jessy Bali
Duran Bathija
Khadija Buhadi
Roland Graber
Rakhima Missidenti
William O'Reilly
Cyrus Samii

Photographers
Barzin Baharlooei
Cemal Emden
Néo Spot
Kristian Skeie
Chérif Tall
Rajesh Vora

Film Crew
Clan Productions: Ladan Anoushfar, Neil Cameron
Dev-TV: Jon Bjorgvinsson, Maximilian Jacobson-Gonzalez, Bernard Robert-Charrue, Kristin Sellefyan, Iwan Wood and Marina Wutholen
Saodat Ismailova

ther contributors to the 2016 Award Cycle
azim Ahmad
dham Al-Sayed
aleed Al-Sayeed
aria Aslam
ancis Carpentier
aima Chemrouk
or Demchenko
aul Dujardin
ainab Faruqi Ali
mar Abdulaziz Hallaj
Hadi Jazairy
eran Long
ad Malick
ca Molinari
rshid Moussavi
nir Pasic
usuf Patel
ancis Rambert
ai Rigby
an Strauwen
an Tümertekin

s well as the 644 nominators and 401 architects
ho submitted projects.

Architecture and Plurality
Aga Khan Award for Architecture 2016

This monograph has been conceived by Mohsen Mostafavi and Farrokh Derakhshani on behalf of the Steering Committee of the 2016 Aga Khan Award for Architecture.

Project descriptions were assembled by Suneeta Gill and Pamela Johnston, based on reports prepared by the 2016 On-Site Project Reviewers.

Documentation materials have been compiled and reviewed by Nadia Siméon.

Copy-Editor: Pamela Johnston
Design: Integral Lars Müller
Printing and Binding: Kösel, Altusried-Krugzell, Germany
Paper: 150 gsm, Lessebo Design Smooth White

Published by
Lars Müller Publishers
Zurich, Switzerland
www.lars-mueller-publishers.com

Aga Khan Award for Architecture
PO Box 2049
1211 Geneva 2
Switzerland
www.akdn.org/architecture

ISBN 978-3-03778-523-2

Printed in Germany

Also available at Lars Müller Publishers:

Architecture is Life
Aga Khan Award for Architecture 2013
ISBN 978-3-03778-378-8

Implicate & Explicate
Aga Khan Award for Architecture 2010
ISBN 978-3-03778-242-2